HOW DO
YOU SPELL
GOD?

"A beautiful, wise, and eminently readable book that will appeal to anyone of any age."
—Mary Higgins Clark

"Gellman and Hartman set out to do the impossible and have succeeded. They have written a book about religion that young people will enjoy reading and learn much from. I salute their achievement."
—Rabbi Harold Kushner
author of *When Bad Things Happen to Good People*

"*How Do You Spell God?* offers a most beautiful service to children everywhere. It answers their penetrating questions about God with clarity-light and wisdom-delight and it teaches them to love and respect all the different branches of the world family of religions."
—Sri Chinmoy
author of *Beyond Within*

"Monsignor Hartman and Rabbi Gellman write with passion and intelligence. In an age when religious illiteracy among the young (and their elders!) is so widespread, one praises their effort as well as their unique capacity to speak the language of young people."
—(Rev.) Theodore M. Hesburgh
President Emeritus
University of Notre Dame

"Islamic traditions encourage people to 'seek knowledge from the cradle 'til the grave,' and to 'seek knowledge even if it was as far as China'! The tremendous amount of knowledge presented by Monsignor Hartman and Rabbi Gellman in this book will indeed challenge us to seek further knowledge throughout life, even if distant journeys are required."
—Al-Haaj Ghazi Y. Khankan
President
National Council of Islamic Affairs

How Do You Spell God?

Answers to the Big Questions
from Around the World

RABBI MARC GELLMAN &
MONSIGNOR THOMAS HARTMAN

illustrated by Jos. A. Smith

WITH A FOREWORD BY
HIS HOLINESS THE DALAI LAMA

MORROW JUNIOR BOOKS
NEW YORK

Pen and ink were used for the illustrations.
The text type is 13.5-point Centaur.

Printed in the United States of America.

Book design by PIXEL PRESS

1 2 3 4 5 6 7 8 9 10

Library of Congress Cataloging-in-Publication Data
Gellman, Marc.
    How do you spell God? / by Rabbi Marc Gellman and Monsignor Thomas
Hartman.
       p. cm.
    ISBN 0-688-13041-0
    1. Religions—Juvenile literature.   2. Religion—Juvenile
literature.   3. God—Juvenile literature.   [1. Religions.]
I. Hartman, Thomas.   II. Title.
BL92.G45 1995
200—dc20   94-28770   CIP AC

For:

Herman and Sheila Hartman and Sol and Rosalie Gellman, who taught us how to ask the big questions and wait for the big answers.

FOREWORD

All the world's religious traditions are similar because they help us become better human beings. For centuries, millions of people have found peace of mind in their own religious tradition. Today, the world over, we can find followers of many faiths giving up their own welfare in order to help others. I believe that this wish to work for the happiness of others is the most important goal of all religious practice.

Human beings naturally possess different interests. So, it is not surprising that we have many different religious traditions with different ways of thinking and behaving. But this variety is a way for everyone to be happy. If we have a great variety of food, we will be able to satisfy different tastes and needs. When we only have bread, the people who eat rice are left out. And the reason those people eat rice is that rice is what grows best where they live.

Because the important point of all the different religious traditions is to be helpful, we must maintain harmony and respect between them. This will benefit not only the followers of each religion, but will make our own neighborhoods and countries more peaceful. To do this we need to understand something about the world's different religions. Therefore, I am very happy that my friend Rabbi Marc Gellman and Monsignor Thomas Hartman have written this book that explains in a clear and easy way what the world's religions are about.

For most of us, our religion depends on our family and where we were born and grew up. Usually I think it is better not to change that. However, the more we understand of each other's ways, the more we can learn from each other. And the more easily we can develop respect and tolerance in our own lives and in our behavior towards each other. This will certainly help to increase peace and friendship throughout the world, which is one of the aims of all major religions.

His Holiness the Dalai Lama

Acknowledgments

—

A book of this scope made us even more grateful to and dependent upon the wise advice of our teachers and friends and fellow spiritual seekers who have generously shared their wisdom with us throughout the creation and editing of this book. It is not just modesty that compels us to admit that the mistakes in this book are our responsibility and not theirs; it is the truth! For their help along the way we gratefully thank Gil Meilander; Sri Chinmoy; all our friends at the Islamic Center of Long Island, especially Ghazi Khankan and Faroque Khan; George Weigel; Diana Cutler; Bob Lord; and Gypsy da Silva.

Our editor, David Reuther, was also our teacher, and the entire staff at Morrow Junior Books was our strong right arm. Again, any weakness in the left arm is our fault.

Contents

—

1. What's a Religion?   I
2. How Are Religions the Same?   5
3. How Are Religions Different?   11
4. How Do You Spell God?   22
5. What Question Does Each Religion Want to
   Answer the Most?   26
6. Who Are the Big Teachers?   47
7. What Are the Holy Books?   61
8. Where Are the Holy Places?   71
9. When Are the Holy Days?   79
10. What Are the Holy Times in My Life?   99
11. Why Do Religions Split Up?   114
12. Who Works for God?   126
13. How Do You Build a House for God?   137
14. Can I Talk to God?   145

Contents

15. Why Does Bad Stuff Happen to Good Folks?   159
16. How Should We Live?   164
17. What Happens After We Die?   179
18. What Are Some of the Bad Things in Religions?   186
19. What Are Some of the Terrific Things in Religions?   194

Consumer Warning!

Some of the parts of this book are very serious, but some parts of this book have been determined by independent experts to be funny.

We don't exactly know how this happened, but when we found out, we did want to warn you right away. So, if you are the kind of person who believes that religion is *never* funny; if you are the kind of person who thinks that it is quite all right for religions to make you cry, and feel bad about things, but never all right for religions to make you laugh . . . then this might be the wrong book for you.

If you do read this book and you find something in it that seems to you to be disrespectful or funny in the wrong way, we deeply apologize. We only want people to follow the way to goodness and God in joy.

God bless!
Rabbi Marc Gellman and Monsignor Tom Hartman

How Do You Spell God?

CHAPTER I

What's a Religion?

A religion is a bunch of big answers to the really big questions. Nobody wants to learn about religions just because there are religions out there. We want to learn about religions because we want to get the answers to the big questions. When we find out that religions have real good answers to real big questions—*"Wham!"*—that is when we want to learn about religions. Now, there are questions that all religions answer and questions that only some religions answer. The way we see it, there are four big questions all the religions in the world try to answer:

1. "What's our place in the world?"
2. "How can we live the right way?"
3. "How do we pray?"
4. "What happens to us after we die?"

If something answers these questions, it's a religion; if it doesn't, it isn't! If these questions matter to you, then you will want to know about religions. If they don't, you won't. You see, these are the biggest, most important questions we ask in our lives. These questions are the reasons religions started up, and they are the reasons religions keep going. We need to know the answers to the really big questions.

In this book we don't teach you that only one religion has the right answers to these questions. What we believe is that *all* the religions of the world have some good answers to these questions. We have decided that all the religions of the world have something wonderful and true and good to teach us about the big questions.

Think of a diamond. When you look at a diamond, there isn't just one right way. Every side of a diamond shows you a special and different sparkle. It's the same with religions. Each religion in the world is like a diamond. Each religion sparkles in its own way.

It's the same when you think about your parents. When you say that you love your parents, you don't mean that they are the only good parents in the whole world. What you mean is that you have learned more from your parents than from anyone else, that you are close to them in a special way, that you will always love them, and that you will tell the stories of their lives to the children of your children. Our religion is like that. We are close to our religion in a special way. We never get tired of its stories, but we are always ready to hear a good story from another religion that other people love just the way we love ours.

One of us (Marc Gellman) is a rabbi, and one of us (Tom Hartman) is a priest. We love our religions. We don't want to change our religions. We want to follow the teachings of our own religions and keep those teachings alive. We don't want all the religions to melt down into one big religion. This would be boring and would make the world very dull. It would be like having just one baseball team, or just one band, or just one painter, or just one flavor of ice cream. The different religions in the world help to give the world its color and spice, its rhythm and its smiles. How could you not want to know about all that?

If you live long enough, you will meet somebody who hates religions. One of the things the people who hate religions say a lot is, "Religions divide people and teach them to hate each other." This is ridiculous, and here's what we say to people who don't like religions: "Look around this world! Look at the people who are doing good stuff, the people who are giving out soup to hungry folks who have no money to pay for the soup, the people who are building houses for folks who have no money to pay for the houses, the people who are taking care of little children who nobody wants to take care of—the good people. Can't you see that lots of these people doing good stuff have a religion that taught them to do it?"

Then we say, "Look around this world at the people who are doing bad stuff. The people who kill folks for no reason, the people who hurt folks for 'fun,' the people who beat up people because of the color of their skin, the people who cheat and lie and steal and throw their beer cans out of the windows of their cars—the bad people. Can't you see that none of these people learned how to do that bad stuff from a religion?"

We know that you can be a good person even if you have no religion. You can do good things not because you learned them from a religion but because you just learned them from good people. We know that there are creeps in religion and good folks who aren't religious, but here's the thing: The teachings of religion are behind all the good things people do.

The main thing is to do good stuff and not to worry so much about where it comes from. But when somebody says that religions divide people and teach them to hate each other, you should stand up and tell them that they are full of baloney. If they don't want to listen to you, just pick yourself up and go somewhere else where the good people are trying to fix the world with other good people who don't really care that much how they got to be good.

Now, there is just one last thing. We know that there are some folks who teach that their religion is the only right religion. We have no problem with folks who believe that their religion is right. We have no problem with folks who believe that their religion is more right than any other religion. We *do* have a problem with people who believe that they have the *only* right religion and then go out and hurt other people because of it. If you hurt people because of what you think your religion teaches, it just proves that you never learned what your religion *really* teaches.

There is an old story about a king who had a beautiful ring and three sons. Each son wanted the ring. One day the king died and left three rings for his three sons. He also left a note that said, "My dear sons, one of these rings is real and two of these rings are fakes. The way you will know who has the real ring is that the one with the real ring will be kind and generous to all people." Each of the sons spent the rest of his life being good to prove that he had the real ring. It's the same with religions. The way to show that your religion is true is not to yell and scream about it. The way to show that your religion is true is to live it.

CHAPTER 2

How Are Religions the Same?

—

Religions are the same because they all answer the same questions. We already gave you our list of four questions all the religions in the world ask and all the religions in the world answer. Let's look at those questions a little closer now.

"What's Our Place in the World?"

All religions teach us what we are supposed to be doing with our life here on planet earth. Religions do this by telling us stories about the world and about wise people who lived in it before us. Some religions tell us that our place is in a world made by one God. Other religions tell us that our place is in a world made by many gods, and a few religions teach us that we are in a world with no gods at all. But all the religions end up by teaching us about our place in the world. Finding our place in the world means finding the meaning of life.

The stories that help us find our place in the world are stories that are supposed to change us. When we hear the stories of our religion, we are supposed to become better in a deep way. Becoming better in a deep way has a name, a big name: *salvation.* Salvation means "being saved."

Religions save us. "Save us from what?" you might ask. Well, it's not crocodiles! Religions save us from doing the wrong thing. Doing the wrong thing is called *sin.* Religions save us from ignorance, which is not knowing the right thing to do. Religions save us from suffering, which means being miserable all the time. Religions save us. That is one of the big things religions do.

The stories are not what save us. The stories are the way religions teach us how to be saved. Being saved is what finding our place in the world is really all about.

"How Can We Live the Right Way?"

If you were the only person in the whole world, you would not need to know how to live the right way. It would be just you alone, and you could live any way you wanted. But once there are two people, you need to know how to live with the other person in the world. Religion was the first way that people learned how to live with each other in a good and kind way. We think that religion is still the best way that people learn how to live together.

What is amazing to us is that religions all over the world teach the same right way to live. Religions from the mountains and religions from the valleys, religions from the deserts and religions from the forests, old religions and young religions—all religions have many of the same ideas of how to live the right way. All religions teach us to help people whenever we can help them. All religions teach us to play fair and not to hit or kill or steal or cheat. All religions teach us we should be forgiving and cut people some slack when they mess up because someday we will mess up too. All religions teach us to love our families, to respect our parents, and to make new families when we grow up. This is amazing. Religions everywhere have nearly the same ideas of how to live the right way.

Part of living the right way is learning what to do if you don't, what to do when you make a mistake. Religions teach us how to pick ourselves up and start all over again when we do the wrong thing; religions are always there to help us get back to living the right way.

Religions have different names for their teachings about the right way to live. Taoists call their teachings *Tao* (pronounced *dao*). Jews call it *Torah*. Buddhists call their teachings *dharma*. Hindus call it *Yoga*. Christians call it *Gospel*. Muslims call it *al-Quran*.

These teachings about the right way to live are like a path. The religions say that if we live in the right way and stay on the path, we will be all right, but if we go off the path, we mess up the world and mess up ourselves. All religions teach that staying on the path of living the right way changes the world just as much as it changes us. Religions also teach that living the right way protects the world just like the way protects us. The path is like a great wind that carries us along. The path is like the sails of a great ship making its way through the sea to someplace far away that is still home. The path leads us to the best thing there is.

"How Do We Pray?"

Prayers are the way religions teach us to speak the words that are in our hearts, not just on our lips. When we are filled with wonder at something beautiful in the world, prayers turn that wonder into words that go out as a thank-you note to God. When

7

we are scared about something, prayers turn our fear into words that make the fear get smaller. When we need something really important (not a bike or a VCR) and we do not know where to turn, prayers give voice to that need. Prayers also help us keep up our hope that what we need will come to us soon, and that what we *really* need we already have. Prayers are the ways we turn our inside feelings into words for God.

Prayers are also ways for us to say how happy we are that it is a certain time of the year. Springtime and harvest time and the time when something big happened long ago; all these times are remembered in prayers. They are never forgotten, because of the prayers.

Prayers help us to teach the story of our religion to our kids. Prayers are like little lessons about God and the world. Each prayer teaches something real important and makes that teaching stick.

Prayers are the way religious people first learned to sing. Prayers can be spoken or said silently or written down on a piece of paper, but prayers are really meant to be sung. Prayers are the songs of people singing "I love you" to God and to the world and to each other.

Prayers are also ways that we clean our minds and get to think about deep things and important things. Even religions that do not believe in God believe in prayer for this reason. They use prayers to cleanse the mind, like holy soap. They help people to become wise and free and full of the brightness of knowing what really matters and what is just not real.

All religions have prayers because all religions have people in them, and all people need to give their wonder and their fear, their thanks and their need, their searching and their finding just the right words.

"What Happens to Us After We Die?"

Religions are the way we keep from freaking out about death. Death is the end of life. In a way, death is like a wall at the edge of a garden, and religions are the way we look over that wall. Religions are the way we think about what comes after death, that there is something over the wall. Religions teach us that even though death is definitely the end of our bodies, it is not the end of us.

Even though all the religions teach that there is something after death, they have different ideas of what that something is. Some religions teach that we have a soul, which is a part of us that does not die when our body dies, and after death our soul goes to heaven if we were good in life or to hell if we were bad. Some religions teach that our soul gets put into a new body after we die, and this happens over and over again until we get as good as we can be. Some religions teach that we have no soul but that after we die something goes on in some way.

All these different teachings about what happens after we die give us hope, hope that death is not the end. Hope takes away our fear of death. Giving us hope so that we do not freak out about death is one of the big ways that all the religions help us get through life and face death.

The teaching that death is not the end of us really comes from a deeper hope. That deeper hope is that love never dies. Love is the best thing we know. Love is the only thing we want to last forever, and religions teach us that it does last forever.

CHAPTER 3

How Are Religions Different?

You know how baseball has different divisions for all the teams, but the whole thing is still baseball? Well, it's kind of the same thing for religions. The religions in the world are in different divisions, but it's still all religion. This is the point: The questions *all* the religions ask and answer are what makes them the same. The questions only *some* of the religions ask and answer are what makes them different.

The religions in the world are the same in the big ways we learned in the last chapter, but the religions in the world are also different in big ways. Let's look at some of them.

Some Religions Believe in One God, and Some Religions Believe in Skillions of Gods

The difference between believing in one God and believing in many gods is not just numbers. There is something real deep behind this difference. In the religions that believe in many gods, there is no one thing that holds everything in the world together. In the religions that believe in one God, there is.

In religions with many gods, there is no one God who makes the sun and the oak tree, the lion and the octopus all work together and fit together and live by the same rules. This means that in religions where people believe in many gods, it is harder to find one reason why everything works.

In religions with one God, everything that exists was made by that God. Everything fits together in a plan for the universe made by the one God. The religions with many gods explain some things better, and the religions with one God explain other things better. One God makes us look at the way things fit together. Many gods make us think about the way things are different.

The religions that believe in many gods have an easier time explaining the bad stuff in the world than religions that believe in only one God. The many-god religions can say, "Bad stuff comes from the bad gods and good stuff comes from the good gods." It is kind of like *The Wizard of Oz*, where all the bad and spooky stuff comes from the Wicked Witch of the West and all the good stuff comes from the Good Witch of the North.

The one-God religions teach that good comes from God and evil comes from people turning away from God. These religions teach that God has given people the freedom to do good or to do bad. The freedom people have to make bad choices is the place that most of the evil in the world comes from. God is good, but God gave people the freedom to be bad.

The biggest one-God religions are the religions that teach that a man named Abraham was their ancestor. They are Judaism, Christianity, and Islam. The biggest many-gods religions began in India and came out of the oldest religion in India, which is Hinduism.

Some Religions Believe That There Are Gods, and Other Religions Believe That There Are No Gods

Buddhism is a religion that teaches that there is no God in the world. We put Buddhism in this book because even though it does not teach about God, Buddhism does answer the four questions of all religions. It tells us our place in the world, it teaches people how to live the right way, it teaches people about life after death, and it teaches people how to pray.

Buddhism teaches people how to be saved, and the big thing it wants to save people from is ignorance. Buddhists teach that to understand the world, you must understand that nothing is really real. Buddhists teach that when we understand that nothing is really real, we will be free and happy and calm. This being deeply happy and really calm by knowing that nothing is real is called *nirvana.*

People who believe in one God or in many gods may think that without God or gods, you can't teach folks how to live right. But Buddhism does teach folks to live right without talking about God. Buddhism is also peaceful and does not believe in hurting anybody or killing animals for any reason. It takes time to learn what Buddhists are teaching. Teaching that the world is not really real may seem strange, but Buddhism is worth the trouble to understand. Buddhism reminds us that not all the religions in the world need God to get where they are going.

Some Religions Teach That We Are Supposed to Try to Get Free of the World, and Some Religions Teach That We Are Supposed to Change the World

All religions teach us how to get free of the world *and* how to change the world, but each religion picks one or the other and pushes that teaching more.

Buddhism and Hinduism are two religions that teach how to get free of the world. Hindus call getting free of the world *moksha*, which means "getting free of being born again as somebody or something else." When you get moksha you are free from the world, free from having to go to school again or passing math again, free from getting shots or getting sick, free from pain, and free from death. The most important way that moksha makes you free is that it sets you free from being born again as something or somebody else after you die. This idea of being reborn over and over again until you are free is called *reincarnation.*

For Buddhism, getting free of the world is called *enlightenment.* Enlightenment means that you understand why the world is the way it is. Enlightenment means that you understand why there is suffering and pain. Enlightenment means that you understand that nothing is real.

The religions that teach how to change the world believe that the only way for each of us to get free is for *all* of us to get free. The religion that pushes this idea the most is Judaism. Some parts of Christianity and some parts of Islam also teach this idea. A verse from Leviticus teaches the way Judaism wants us to change the world: "Proclaim liberty throughout the land unto all the inhabitants thereof." (Leviticus 25:10) The people who founded America liked this idea so much they put this verse on the Liberty Bell.

Religions that teach us how to live in the world say to the

religions that teach us to get free of the world, "How can you just sit there and let starving people starve and enslaved people stay slaves? We shouldn't just sit around waiting to die and get out of the world. We should do what we can to make the world a better place while we are alive."

The religions that mostly teach us to get free of the world say right back, "Don't be silly. If you think that what you do is going to change the world you are wrong. There *was* suffering in the world. There *is* suffering in the world. And there *will always be* suffering in the world. *Nothing* you can do is going to change that. If you try to change the world by getting everybody free and by getting all the hungry people a good hot meal, you are just going to be frustrated and angry and depressed your whole life. And the sooner you learn that, the calmer, wiser, and happier you will be."

If you grow up in a place where you are taught a live-in-the-world religion, you may think that the get-free-of-the-world religions are wrong because they do not want to change the bad stuff in the world. If you grow up in a place where you are taught a get-free-of-the-world religion, you may think that the live-in-the-world religions are wrong because they make people crazy trying to change things that can't be changed.

The get-free-of-the-world religions all teach that we get born over and over again, and the change-the-world religions teach that this life is our only life. The difference about whether we live one life or many lives is a huge difference in religions. If you believe that you are going to live on forever with God after your body dies and your one life here on earth will decide what happens to you forever and ever, you are going to care *a lot* about what you do in your one turn at bat here in this life. If you believe that you are going to be reborn over and over again, then what you do in the life you are living now is not really all that important because you will have lots of other chances to get it right in your next lives. It's the difference between taking a big test just one time or taking that test over and over again until you get all the answers right. The first way you are going to bite your fingernails and chew your eraser, and the other way you are going to say, "What the hey!"

There are good and bad things about both kinds of religions. The one-time-at-bat religions care a lot about what we do to change this world, because this is our only chance. The over-and-over-again religions don't always care that much about changing the world, but they make people much more calm and less hassled. But both kinds of religions teach people to love each other. Both kinds of religions make for people who do good deeds in the world, but the two kinds of religions are different.

There Are Religions You Can Join and Religions You Can't Join Because You Have to Be Born into Them

To be a part of a tribe, you have to be born into that tribe. You can't just say, "I would like to be an Inuit." If your mom and dad were not Inuit, then you can't be one, no matter what you do. You can buy one of those furry parkas, and you can go out and hunt seals in a kayak, and when you get back to the igloo, the other Inuit will look at you and say, "What the heck are you doing here?" That's the way it is with tribes. You get to be in a tribe because of whom you were born to, not what you believe.

The religions that care more about where you came from than what you believe are what we call *tribal* religions. Tribal religions don't let anybody into the religion unless they are born into it. Other religions let in anybody who believes in what the religion teaches. These are what we call *open* religions. The open religions don't care who your parents were or what your tribe is. The difference between tribal and open religions is one of the big differences in the religions of the world.

Many of the tribal religions are small, because most tribes are small, but there is one huge tribal religion in the world, and it is Hinduism. Hinduism is the religion of the tribes of India. Most Hindus say that you have to be born a Hindu to be a Hindu. The reason for this is that Hindus have a caste system that teaches that different Hindus are born into different levels of Hinduism. A *caste* is your place in the Hindu group.

Today some Hindus are saying that anybody who wants to be a Hindu can be a Hindu. In 1955 the government of India tried to make Hinduism more open by passing a law that said that anybody who wants to be a Hindu can be one. But this law is not followed by all Hindus. Hindu teachers told the government of India, "You pick up the garbage and deliver the mail and leave the laws of Hinduism to us."

Christianity is an example of an open religion. Anybody can become a Christian if they believe that Jesus was the son of God who came to earth, died for our sins, and came back from the dead. Now, many folks think that open religions are better than tribal religions, but we think that there are good things about both kinds of religions. Tribal religions are good because they make a real tight fit between religion and how you live. The way the people live in a tribe includes their religion. In open religions, people can sometimes put their religion into one small part of their lives and not connect it to the way they live every day.

The bad part about tribal religions is that they do not give people a choice, and having a choice is a good thing. Open religions are free and let anybody come in who believes that the religion is true. Open religions say, "Here is what we believe. If you believe the same thing, join us. We are glad to have you." That's a nice thing to say.

But sometimes there are bad things about open religions. Some open religions don't just let you join them, they try to force you to join them! Joining a religion is called *converting* to the religion, and a person who changes his or her religion is called a *convert*. Religions that try to get converts can pester you and even sometimes try to force you to join them. When the Native Americans met the Spaniards who sailed over with Columbus, they found out real fast that these Christians were trying to force them to give up their native religions and join up with Christianity. A person who goes out to get converts for a religion is called a *missionary*. Many Christian missionaries were very gentle and kind, but some were real mean and wouldn't take no for an answer.

Judaism is a religion that is part tribal and part open. You can become a Jew two different ways. One way to become a Jew is to be born of a Jewish mother. Some Jews say that it is okay if just your father is Jewish. The other way to become a Jew is to say that you believe in Judaism. So Judaism is an open religion because anybody can join up who wants to, but it is also a tribal religion because if your mom was Jewish, you are also Jewish no matter what you say or what you do or what you believe. You can believe that Judaism is a load of baloney, but if your mom was Jewish, you are still a Jew. In fact, if your mom was Jewish and you grow up and join Christianity and then change your mind and decide to become a Jew again, you don't have to convert back to being a Jew. Judaism says, "Oh, that's all right. Once you are born Jewish you are always Jewish."

One of the real interesting differences between open religions and tribal religions is that open religions are usually started because of the teachings of one single big teacher, but tribal religions begin because of the way a tribe lives. Christianity is an open religion, and it is built around the teachings of Jesus. Buddhism is an open religion, and it is built around the teachings of the Buddha. Islam is an open religion, and it is built around the teachings of Muhammad. You can't separate those religions from those teachers. But Hinduism and Judaism and Shintoism are tribal religions, and they have no one big teacher who started the whole religion. Open religions are more worried about getting the teachings of the one big teacher right, while tribal religions spend more time worrying about living in the right way.

The point is, there are good and bad things about all the religions of the world, no matter how they are the same, no matter how they are different. When you start thinking that all the religions in the world are really the same, go back to the parts of this book that teach you how the religions are different. When you start thinking that all the religions in the world are really different, go back to the parts of this book that teach you how they are the same. We hope you will finish this book with the feeling that each and every religion is wonderful in some special way.

Still, you may wonder just *why* there are so many religions in the world. Here are two ways we thought of to help you understand this:

All the Religions in the World Are Like Different Paths Up the Same Mountain

You know that there is never just *one* way to climb a mountain. If the mountain is real big, there are always lots of paths that get you to the top. Mountains are just too big to have only one way up. It's the same with religions. God is such a big idea, such a big thing, such a big being, that no matter how many ways we try

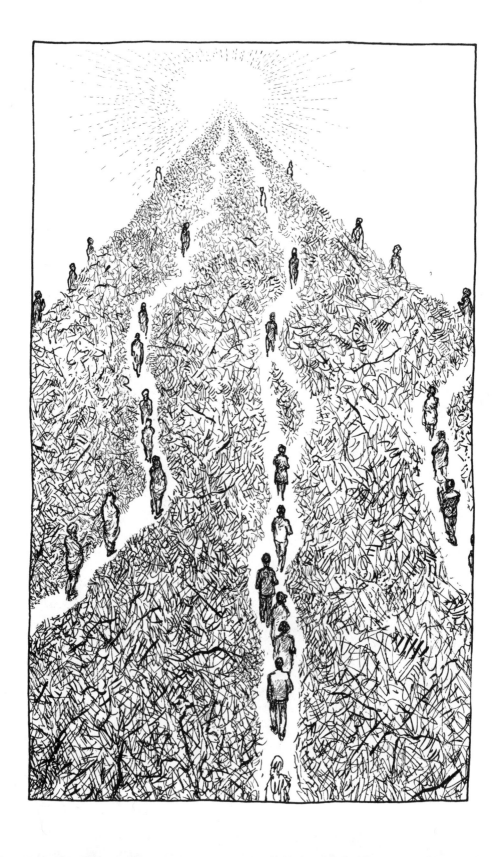

to understand God and God's teachings, there are always more ways.

God is bigger by far than the biggest mountain, and all the religions in the world are like all the different ways up the mountain, like all the different ways we humans have tried to understand God. Thinking that there should be just one religion in the world is like thinking that there should be just one path up every mountain. Why would you ever think that?

All the Religions in the World Are Like Different Parts of a Beautiful Song

Some of the most beautiful music in the world is beautiful because it has different notes, different parts, different sounds, that all fit together to make something beautiful. We call the fitting together of the different parts of a song *harmony.* It is harmony that makes so much music beautiful.

Religion is like this beautiful music. Each religion is like a singer in God's song to the world. Each religion has a part to sing, certain notes to play that fit into the big song that is the song of the universe. And the music we all make together sings about goodness and hope and courage, it sings about love and kindness and wisdom, and it sings about heaven and nature and God. This great song is more beautiful because all the religions of the world are singing different parts of it. The religions are like the instruments in a symphony, like the singers in the chorus.

Enjoy the music of this book, enjoy the scenery from each of the different paths up the mountain. We hope and pray that each of you will become more gentle and forgiving because of the climbing, and because of the singing.

CHAPTER 4

How Do You Spell God?

Why do you have a name? We think you have a name so that people don't have to say "Hey you!" all the time, or so that the letter carrier knows where to put your mail. You need a name so your teacher will know who aced the test. And most of all you need a name so that the person at the bakery will know what to write on the top of your birthday cake with that gooey blue icing. As close as we can figure it, these are the reasons you need a name.

Now, when you think about it, God does not need a name for any of these reasons. Nobody says "Hey you!" to God. God's mailbox is our soul, so we don't have to put a stamp on a letter to get a message to God. God knows everything. And maybe God doesn't like blue icing.

So why does God have a name? It's simple. God doesn't need a name, but *we* need to give God a name because we want to talk about God. If God had no name, we would just have to leave a blank space every time we wanted to write about God, and the whole thing would be very confusing. We also need to give God a name so that we can thank God in our prayers for all the good stuff God has put into our lives.

So let's look at the names that the religions that believe in God give to God. Each name is a lesson.

Muslims say that God's name is *Allah,* which is an Arabic word. Don't forget that the word *God* is only the English name for God (actually the name *God* came to English from the German name for God, which is *Gott).* Muslims teach us a very great thing about God's name. They say that in addition to the name Allah, God has ninety-nine other names. What this means is that we can think up all the names we want to for God, and there will always be more names because God is always more than we can know and more than we can say. It means that almost anything good is the name of God. Some of the ninety-nine names for Allah are: the Wise, the Good, the Merciful, the Compassionate, the One, the Forgiver, the Great, the King, the Holy, the Protector, the Strong, the Hearer, the Judge, the Rewarder, the Watcher, the Answerer, the Loving, the Real, the First, the Far Away, the Real Close, the Maker of Everything Else, and the Light. Our favorite is *al Salam,* "the place where peace comes from." Each one of these is kind of like a nickname for God. Each of these names is a different way of saying what God is or what God does.

Judaism is like Islam. It has many names for God: the Merciful One, our Father, our King, the Forgiver, the Judge, the Holy One Blessed Be He, the Creator, the Saver, the One Who Lives Near Us, the Name, and the Place. Our favorite is *ehyeh asher ehyeh,* which means "I am what I am."

Jews believe that we can't ever pronounce the real name of God. This is to teach us that God is too big to fit into just one name, that we can't ever really know all about God, and also to teach us that we shouldn't use God's holy name just for the heck of it. In the Hebrew Bible, God's name is written with four Hebrew letters that sound sort of like the four English letters Y, H, V, H. When the YHVH name for God comes up in the reading of the Hebrew Bible, Jews don't try to pronounce it. They just substitute another name, *Adonai*, which means "my Lord." There are some Christians who have tried to pronounce the YHVH name as "Yahweh," or as "Jehovah," but Jews don't even try because it is not allowed. For Jews, God's real name is supposed to stay secret.

Christianity teaches that God's main name is the same as the YHVH name in the Hebrew Bible, but Christians divide that name into three parts, called the Trinity.

The first name of God for Christians is "God the Father," which is the name Christians use when they are talking about God making the world and making everything in it.

The second name for God in Christianity is "God the Son," which is the name for Jesus. When Christians use the name Jesus, they are talking about God coming to earth in the form of a human being. This means that Jesus was a person and Jesus was also God. Jesus died on earth to save people from sin, which is doing something against God or people or ourselves. Sin means turning away from God and walking off the path God has shown us.

The third name for God is "the Holy Spirit." This is the name Christians use for God when they are talking about God doing things in the world. The Holy Spirit is also the name for God when we feel that God is very, very close to us.

Many religions have one name for God as the maker of the world and another name for God as the loving hope for the future. The main thing is that all the names of God are naming the same God! A good way to understand this is to think about how you feel about somebody you really love. Even when you are not with them, you still love them and feel their love for you. It's the same with God. Some of the names for God help us to remember that God's love is always with us, even if we can't see it like we can see each other. In fact the best way to see the name of God is to look into the eyes of somebody you love. All the names of God are written in their eyes.

CHAPTER 5

What Question Does Each Religion Want to Answer the Most?

Each religion in the world asks and answers many questions, but in each religion there is one huge question that is the most important question for that religion. The one huge question gives each religion its special flavor the way the pepper or the salt or the garlic or the cheese gives each dish its special taste. Here are some of the religions you will meet in this book, and here are their own special big huge questions that have made each one what it was and what it is and what it will be.

Hinduism

The big huge question of Hinduism is: **"How can I get free of being born over and over again in this world?"**

There are almost 750 million Hindus in the world trying to answer this question, but if you want to find most of them, go to India. Hinduism is the religion of almost nine out of ten people who live in that country. Some religions are so mixed into the history of a country that you can't really divide the religion from the country. Hinduism and India are like that.

For Hindus the big question comes from their believing that we are trapped in this world. What it means to a Hindu to be trapped in the world is that when we die, it is just our bodies that die. Hindus believe that our soul, which they call *atman*, gets stuffed right back into a new body and lives again. This idea is called by a big word, *reincarnation.* Reincarnation means "being born over and over and over and over again."

Hindus teach that the life you live in your new body after you are reborn depends on how good a life you lived in your old body. This teaching is called *karma.* Karma is kind of the Hindu idea of "what goes around comes around." It is the teaching that everything we do changes us and changes what happens to us. The good we do changes us for the better; the bad we do changes us for the worse. If you did good things in your life, you would have good karma. If you have good karma, you might come back after you die as a higher, better person. Maybe you come back as Michael Jordan, or maybe you come back as the President of the United States, or maybe as a king or a queen, or maybe, if you are really good, you will come back as the person who works the scoreboard in baseball games!

If you have bad karma, Hindus teach that you will come back on a lower level of living things. Maybe you come back as a mosquito. Then if you are a good mosquito and only sting bad people, you would have good mosquito karma and come back as a person, and then you would be going back up the ladder of reincarnation. The main thing is that it is your choice to do good and get good karma and move up, or do bad and get bad karma and move down.

Karma is the reason Hindus have a caste system. Hindus call

the castes *varnas.* The highest caste, the highest varna, is the *Brahman* caste. The Brahmans are the priests and kings and thinkers and general big shots. The next varna is the *Kshatriyas,* who are the soldiers. Then comes the *Vaisyas,* who are the farmers and the shopkeepers. The lowest varna is the *Sudras,* who are the workers. Below all four varnas are Hindus who have no caste. They are called "untouchables," because other Hindus were not even supposed to touch them! The government of India passed a law getting rid of this caste, but some Hindus ignore this law.

The caste system is one of the hardest Hindu teachings for people who are not Hindu to understand. Some Hindus do not accept the caste system. Mahatma Gandhi, who was the most famous Hindu of the twentieth century and who helped India get free from the British, did not like the caste system. One of the reasons that Buddhism and Jainism and Sikhism split off from Hinduism is that the people who founded these new religions thought the caste system was cruel and unfair because if you were born into a low caste there was nothing you could do about it in this life.

The idea of karma also makes many Hindus vegetarians. To them, that fried chicken you are eating may be Uncle Herbie born again as a chicken after living a bad life as an accountant! Hindus also believe that cows are holy. There are millions of cows wandering all over the place in India. Cars are always bumping into them, which is bad karma for the driver, bad karma for the cow, and very bad karma for the car's bumpers. What all this means is that your chances of getting a Big Mac or a Whopper in India are not very big.

Reincarnation may sound good to some folks, but it sounds terrible to Hindus. The idea of being born over and over and over again is really depressing to Hindus. Their one big hope is *moksha,* the hope of getting free from being reborn. The question of how to get moksha is the big question that shaped Hinduism.

Hindus teach that there are four paths to moksha, and these paths are called *margas* or *yogas.* The first path is through what we know. This is called *jnana yoga.* This path gets you free by thinking and studying and understanding how everything in the world works. The second path is through what we feel. This is called *bhakti yoga.* This path gets you free by prayer. The third path is through what we do, and this is called *karma yoga.* This path gets you free by doing good deeds in the world.

There is also a path through meditation and bending your body and learning how to breathe in a special way. This is called *hatha yoga.* Many folks who are not Hindus meditate or do hatha yoga just to feel better and to keep their bodies from getting stiff and making funny noises when they get up out of bed. Meditation and hatha yoga are great Hindu gifts to the world. Meditation clears your mind and makes you feel better. It is kind of like resting when you are awake. The Hindus know that you can't take care of your soul if you don't also take care of your body. Reminding us that our bodies are a part of our religion is one of the best parts of Hinduism.

The margas get you free by taking you out of yourself and letting your mind get free first, and then your body will get free later. The main thing about the margas is that each one is very intense, and the other thing about the margas is that each person has his or her own way to get free. A path that works for one person will not work for another person. You just have to find your path and then ease on down the road.

One of the main teachings of Hinduism is that the world is full of gods. Most Hindus believe that there are three main gods who kind of boss all the other gods around. There is the god who made the world, whose name is Brahma. There is the god who keeps everything that Brahma made from falling apart, and his name is Vishnu. And then there is the spooky god who kills things, and his name is Shiva. These three big gods and the skillions of little gods give Hindus a huge choice of gods to whom to pray and bring gifts.

Even though Hindus believe in many gods, they also believe that all the gods are part of a single big truth about the world. Their holy book teaches, "Truth is one and the wise ones call it by many names."

Buddhism

The big huge question of Buddhism is, **"How can I find enlightenment?"** Enlightenment means knowing what is really really true about the whole universe. Enlightenment is called *nirvana* by Buddhists.

Buddhism is a religion that developed out of Hinduism about 2,500 years ago, so its big question is like the big question of Hinduism, and enlightenment is kind of like moksha. Both of them get us out of being reborn over and over again, and both of them get us free of the world. The difference is that for Hindus, we have a soul in us that is real, and that gets free through moksha. In Buddhism, nothing is really real, including our souls, and learning this is what gets us nirvana.

There are about 160 million Buddhists in the world who are trying to become enlightened. There are many names for an enlightened person: Buddha, bodhisattva, or arhat. Siddhartha Gautama was the first person to find enlightenment. He was the first Buddha and the best Buddha. It is hard to explain what you have to do to be a Buddha. Being a Buddha is much more than just going to school, getting an A in every subject, having no tardies and no overdue library books. Being a Buddha means not just being smart, it means being wise. Smart is when you know

what is true; wise is when you know what really matters. Buddhas are both smart and wise.

Siddhartha Gautama lived in India. It was the new things in his teachings that made his followers leave Hinduism and start a new religion. One of the Buddha teachings was that the caste system in Hinduism was wrong. For the Buddha, your caste was not important. What was important to the Buddha was how you lived and what you understood about getting free.

The teachings of the Buddha are called *dharma.* The Buddhists monks who live by the dharma of the Buddha are called the *sangha.* The thing that all Buddhists say that makes them Buddhist is this: "To be safe I go to the Buddha. To be safe I go to the dharma. To be safe I go to the sangha." This is called the Three Refuges. The Buddha is the Buddha. The dharma is the teachings of the Buddha. And the sangha is the group of Buddhist monks who keep the teachings and take care of the Buddhists who are not monks.

After the Buddha, Asoka, who was an emperor of India about 2,300 years ago, tried to make all of India Buddhist, but Hinduism was just too strong. After Asoka, Buddhism became a very small religion in India but a big religion in China and Japan and in southeast Asia. Buddhism in the south of Asia is called *Theravada* Buddhism. You can find this kind of Buddhism in Sri Lanka, Myanmar, Thailand, Vietnam, Laos, and Cambodia. Buddhism in the north of Asia is called *Mahayana* Buddhism. This branch is in Nepal, Sikkim, China, Korea, and Japan. The branch of Buddhism in Tibet and Mongolia and parts of Siberia is called *Tantrayana* Buddhism. In Japan there is a kind of Buddhism called *Zen.*

Each part of Buddhism has a different name for a person who has reached nirvana. In Theravada Buddhism the enlightened one is called an *arhat;* in Mahayana Buddhism, a *bodhisattva;* in Tantrayana Buddhism, a *siddha;* and in Zen Buddhism a *roshi.* The holy people who have reached nirvana are at the end of the road;

they are the tip of the top. Even so, every person who has reached nirvana since the Buddha first reached nirvana is different from the Buddha. They all got to nirvana because they learned the truth from the Buddha. The Buddha got that way because he figured everything out himself.

The head of the Buddhists in Tibet is the Dalai Lama. A Lama is a Buddhist monk in Tibet, and a Dalai Lama is the head monk. The lamas believe that there is really only one Dalai Lama who keeps getting reborn over and over again after he dies. After the death of an old Dalai Lama, a new Dalai Lama is picked from all the Tibetan Buddhist children by looking at special signs. One of the signs of a Dalai Lama is that he is a child who picks out the things of the old Dalai Lama from a pile of things that look the same. The present Dalai Lama did this at age five, and that is how he got picked.

Today the present Dalai Lama can't go home to Tibet and lead Buddhism there because the Chinese Communists don't want him making trouble for them. We hope that this will change soon. It would be nice to see the Dalai Lama back in Tibet and say to him, "Hello, Dalai, it's so nice to have you back where you belong!"

The teaching about nirvana is given to us in Buddhism in four parts. These are called "the Four Noble Truths." These are the four big things that the Buddha found out about the world that helped him get to nirvana. Noble Truth #1, called *dukka*, is that life is full of suffering. Noble Truth #2, called *samudaya*, is that the suffering comes from wanting too much stuff in the world. Noble Truth #3, called *nirodha*, is that we can get rid of suffering by not wanting so much. Noble Truth #4 is called the *middle path*. The middle path is the path you need to walk on to get rid of suffering. This path is in the middle (of course!) between living a life of whoopee! and living a life where you give up almost everything. Not too rich, not too poor, not too fast, not too slow—that is the middle path.

The middle path is also called the Eightfold Path, because it has eight things you must do to get free of suffering and into nirvana. They are: seeing things the right way, hoping for the right things, saying the right things, doing the right things, working in the right way, always trying in the right way, thinking in the right way, and meditating in the right way.

In Buddhism anybody can walk the Eightfold Path and get free by getting into nirvana, but Buddhists believe that the Buddhist monks have a much better shot at nirvana than the other Buddhists. By the way, the rules about being a monk are pretty strict. If you are not a Buddhist monk, you can get married, but you can't kill anything, you can't lie, you can't steal, you can't do crazy stuff, and you can't drink or smoke. If you decide to be a Buddhist monk, you can't do all these things *plus* you can't get married or have a job, you can't eat after noon on any day, you can't go to movies or theme parks or ride on bump 'em cars, you can't wear perfume, you can't sleep on a big soft comfortable bed, and you can't take money for anything.

As a monk you also can't own much. You can own one belt, one bowl for begging, one razor, one needle, and one water strainer. Anything given to you is owned by the group of all the monks, the *sangha.* As a Buddhist monk you can only have three robes. The robe you wear tells people what country you are from. In Sri Lanka Buddhist monks wear orange robes. In Vietnam the monks wear dark brown robes. In Japan the Zen Buddhist monks wear black robes. Tibetan monks wear mauve robes. There are 227 rules for Buddhist monks. The monk rules are called the *patimokkha.* Buddhist monks say the patimokkha every two weeks to check out if they have broken a rule.

One of the main teachings of Buddhism is that everything in the world is not real. Buddhists know that everything we see and touch is sort of real. They know that if you are hungry, you can eat a real apple or real cookie, but Buddhists teach that deep down, *nothing* is really real.

The reason nothing is really real is that everything comes from something else, and so everything depends on everything else. You can't have a son without having a father first, but you can't have a father without a grandfather, and so on back and back. Buddhists teach that everything depends on everything else, so nothing is real all by itself. For Buddhists, God is not real, just like the world is not real. Buddhists have a word for everything not being really real deep down, and that word is *sunya.*

One way to try to understand what the Buddhists are getting at is to think about mirages. You know that a mirage is something you see, but it is not really real. Well, the Buddhist teaching of sunya is sort of like teaching that everything we see is a mirage. Another way to understand this is to think of an echo. An echo of a voice is real, but it is not the voice and so it is not really real. Buddhists teach that everything is like a mirage or like an echo. We know it is hard to understand the Buddhist idea that nothing is really real. Trees and dogs and cats all seem real, and they are real. But for Buddhists they are not *really* real.

The Mahayana Buddhists believe in something that is sort of like God. They call it *tathata,* which means the "One Truth" or the "Law of the Universe," or "suchness." This is not really God, but it is closer to an idea of God than we find in Theravada Buddhism, which really has nothing but sunya.

It's all right if you don't understand this exactly. When you learn about other religions and other people's teachings, some stuff is just going to be real hard to understand. That's the way it is when you are trying to learn something completely different from what you are used to. Just keep trying. Stretching your muscles makes them stronger, and stretching your mind makes it stronger too.

Confucianism

The big question of Confucianism is, **"How can I live by the Way of Heaven?"** The Way of Heaven is like a path we walk on for our whole life. It is the power in the world that runs the world. The Way of Heaven is not God. It is more like a force in the world, like gravity. If we respect the power of the force, we will live a good life, and if we go against the force, we will live a bad life.

The person who taught all this was Confucius, who was a teacher and holy man right up there with Muhammad, Jesus, Buddha, and Moses. Confucius lived in China about 2,550 years ago. He came from a poor family, but he studied hard, and he taught people about how to live in a good way, the Way of Heaven. Confucianism is the oldest religion from China.

Confucius taught that people should be kind to others. He called this *jen*. He taught that people should not go yelling and screaming all over the place and doing stupid things that make them look like jerks. He taught people to be modest and quiet and always to try to do the thing in between two extremes. This kind of life would make a person noble, which he called *chun tzu*. Confucius did not write down his teachings, so most of what we know about him comes from the writings of his students. There is a book with most of his teachings called the Analects of Confucius.

Confucius taught people to respect their ancestors and light candles for them and give them gifts, even though the ancestors could not take the gifts because they were dead. These rituals to show respect for ancestors are called *li*. Confucius also taught people to respect the emperor of China and to be good servants of the emperor.

Taoism

The big huge question of Taoism (which is pronounced *DOW-ism*) is similar to the big huge question of the other old Chinese religion, Confucianism. Taoists ask: **"How can I live my life according to the tao?"** The tao is like the Way of Heaven of Confucianism. The tao is the force for goodness in the world. We can live with the force or against the force, but living against the force will only bring us bad news and make us always sing the blues. The tao is like a river. If your life goes along with the tao, it will be easy, and you will be wise. If you go against the river, you will always be paddling fast, and you will never get anywhere. Taoism teaches that if you get wise and go with the way of the tao, you can live pretty much forever. All the teachings of Taoism are meant to answer the question of how to get your life squared up with the tao of the world.

Taoism believes in millions of gods, but it also teaches that there is one main god, named Yu Huang. Taoism has priests, and you cannot be a priest unless your father is a priest.

Taoism comes from the teachings of two great Chinese holy men. One of them was a teacher named Lao Tzu, and the other was a teacher named Chuang Tzu. People say that Lao Tzu lived at the same time as Confucius, but nobody is really sure about Lao Tzu's life. Lao Tzu wrote a book called the *Tao Te Ching*, which is the teachings of Taoism. Chuang Tzu lived about 2,300 years ago. Chuang Tzu was the main teacher of Taoism to lots of people in China.

Shinto

Shinto is the main religion of Japan, but it comes from Chinese religions. The name *Shinto* comes from the Chinese words *shen tao,* which mean "the way of the gods." Shinto is also about tao. It is also about living in the right way in the world. Just like the religions of China, Shinto is kind of a combination of some of the teachings of Buddhism and Confucianism and Taoism along with the worship of ancestors that is a big deal all through China and Japan.

So the big huge question of Shintoism is, **"How can I live in the way of the tao and also give respect to my ancestors?"** The souls of dead ancestors are called *kami.* The kami are everywhere. Nature is full of kami. The special tree planted in front of a Shinto holy place is called *kami gi,* which means "tree god." Shinto teaches that whenever a person dies, he or she becomes a kami.

In most Shinto homes there is something called the *kami dana,* which is a home shrine. The shrine looks like a little dollhouse and is shaped like the big Shinto shrines. You bring salt and rice and water to the shrine for your grandpa or grandma who has died and turned into a kami. Some days you bring fruit, and some days you bring *sake,* which is rice wine. In some houses they keep a little light on in front of the kami dana all the time.

The main god of all the millions of gods for Japan is the sun god, whose name is Amaterasu. Some Shinto teachings say that the emperor of Japan is a kami, a god, who came from Amaterasu. This teaching made some Japanese people worship the emperor, but now this has changed. Lots of Japanese people—including the current emperor—believe that the emperor is just a person, not a god.

Judaism

The big huge question of Judaism is, **"How can we keep the covenant God has made with us?"** The covenant is called *brit* in Hebrew, and it means the deal that God made with the Jewish people forever and ever, starting with Abraham. God's part of the covenant is to take care of the world and all the people in it. The Jewish people's part in the covenant is to do good deeds, called *gemilut hasadim*, which show that we can love each other just the way God loves us. Jews also teach that praying to God and thanking God for all our blessings is a part of the covenant. Praying is called *avodah*. The covenant is also kept alive by studying and teaching the words of the Bible and the words of the rabbis who explained the Bible. This study is called *talmud torah*.

Judaism began about 3,800 years ago, which makes it just about the oldest religion in the world. Abraham lived about 3,800 years ago. Moses lived about 3,200 years ago. King David lived about 3,000 years ago, and Daniel lived about 2,300 years ago.

The Hebrew Bible and the Talmud are the holy books of the Jews. The Bible was finished about 2,300 years ago, and the Talmud was finished about 1,500 years ago. Some people call the Hebrew Bible "the Old Testament," but Jews don't like that name, because they don't think of their Bible as the "old" part of the Bible. They think that the Hebrew Bible is the whole ball of wax. So Jews call the Old Testament the Hebrew Bible, and they call the New Testament the New Testament.

Judaism was the first religion to teach this big teaching: *There is just one God, who is real mighty and real good. This one God made everything in the world, listens to our prayers, gave us teachings so that we would know how to do the right thing, and when we die takes our souls to heaven (unless we lived like complete jerks).*

This teaching went right from Judaism to Christianity and to Islam, which were the two big religions that came out of Judaism. Christianity and Islam added to this big Jewish teaching, but they did not take away very much from this idea that Judaism gave to the world.

Judaism is a very important religion, even though there are only about 12 million Jews in the world today. Before World War II there were 18 million Jews in the world, but Adolf Hitler and the Nazis killed 6 million Jews as well as 5 million other people in concentration camps during the war. This huge murder of the Jews and other people is called the Holocaust.

Because of the Holocaust and because of the small number of Jews in the world today, many Jews wonder if God has kept the covenant. "How could God let so many Jews die?" they ask. We will talk more about evil in the world in a later chapter, but in short what we think is that God never promised to stop the evil that people do. God promised to love us no matter what evil we do to each other, and God also promised to give a way to live that will get rid of evil if we live that way. The question of the Holocaust is not "Where was God?" but "Where were all the good people who could have stopped it?" The covenant is just a choice, a choice between life and death, between good and evil, between blessing and curse. God says it plainly in the Bible: "Choose life that you and your children might live."

Even though Judaism is small, if you add up all the Jews (about 12 million) and all the Christians (about a billion and a half) and all the Muslims (about a billion), you will see that most of the people in the world today believe that the big Jewish teaching is true.

Jews have a deep love for the land of Israel, even though most Jews don't live there. The way Jews feel about Israel is closest to the way Hindus feel about India. They feel that Israel is not just *their* place, it's a *holy* place. They feel that Jerusalem is the place where heaven and earth kiss. Hindus feel the same way about the Ganges River.

Israel is more than just a holy place for the Jews. After the Holocaust, it was very important for Jews to know that there was a safe place to go to in times of trouble. The State of Israel is that place for Jews all over the world.

Christianity

The big huge question of Christianity is, **"How can I love the way Jesus loved?"** In fact, nobody can love the way Jesus loved because Jesus was God, and the love of Jesus is the love of God. But because of Jesus, Christians are always trying to love other people as much as they can and as hard as they can. All this happens because of the big huge question that Christians ask, and Christians ask that question because of the life and death and love of Jesus.

People talk about Jesus Christ, but "Christ" was not Jesus' last name. Christ is a title, like president or general. Christ is the Greek word for the Hebrew word *moshiach,* which means "Messiah," and Messiah is the Jewish name for a messenger from God. Christians believe that Jesus was the Messiah. So really his name is Jesus the Christ.

The death of Jesus was as big a gift to the world as the life of Jesus. Jesus' death wiped out the sin that came into the world when Adam and Eve disobeyed God by eating the forbidden apple in the Garden of Eden. (Actually it was probably a fig, but "forbidden fig" does not sound as good as "forbidden apple.") The death of Jesus takes away the sins of the world, and the way real Christians give thanks for this tremendous gift of love and suffering from Jesus is by loving all people.

The big teaching of Jesus is that God is love. Jesus taught people not to love just their parents and their friends but even to love their enemies. Jesus loved his enemies, and many of his friends could never figure that out.

Jesus also taught about the Kingdom of God. The Kingdom of God is both a place and a way of living. It begins when you live the way God wants you to live here on earth, and it gets even better when your body dies and your soul goes to heaven.

The holy books of Christianity are called the New Testament. Christians believe that the New Testament is from God. They also believe that the Hebrew Bible is from God. When Jews talk about the Bible they mean the Hebrew Bible. When Christians talk about the Bible they mean the Hebrew Bible plus the New Testament.

Jesus' message and his life were so strong that people took the stories of his life and his death and his being raised from the dead to all the parts of the world. There is no person whose life has changed the lives of more people than Jesus. Nobody else is even close.

There are today over a billion and a half Christians in the world. That makes Christianity the biggest religion in the world. Think of it this way: One out of every three people on earth is a Christian! Some Christians are called Roman Catholics (even if they don't live in Rome). Some Christians are called Protestants, which includes Methodists, Baptists, Presbyterians, Lutherans, Evangelicals, Pentecostals, Quakers, and others. Some Christians are called Anglicans. And some Christians are called Orthodox, including Greek, Russian, Armenian, Byzantine, Antiochean, Ethiopian, and Coptic.

Islam

The big huge question of Islam is, **"How can I give my life to God?"** The people who ask this question are called Muslims. Some people call them Moslems, but if you are Muslim, you don't like to be called a Moslem.

The name *Islam* is really a word that includes the big question of Muslims. The word *Islam* comes from the Arabic word for peace, *salam*, which is almost the same as the Hebrew word for peace, *shalom*. For Muslims the name of their religion means "giving your life to God in a peaceful way." What a great way to name your religion!

Islam finds ways to give our lives to God, whom they call *Allah*. Allah is the Arabic word for "God" plus the Arabic word for "the." So Allah does not just mean God. Allah really means "the God." When Muslims speak of Allah, they are talking about the same God that Jews call Adonai and Christians call God, not sort of the same God, *exactly* the same god!

Muslims believe that the book called the Quran (not, as it's often spelled, the Koran) is the teaching that God gave to Muhammad through the angel Gabriel. The Quran is written in Arabic and is read by Muslims every day, and some of the people in the Bible are also in the Quran. Muslims believe that everything in the Bible came from God and everything in the Quran came from God. They believe that the Quran is the last word from God and that Muhammad is the last prophet. A prophet is a messenger from God. They call Muhammad "the seal of the prophets" (in Arabic, *chatam al'anbiya*), which means that Muhammad is the last messenger from God we will ever need.

There are five main parts to the way Muslims give over their lives to Allah: They pray five times a day while bowing down and facing their holy city of Mecca; they try to travel to the holy city of Mecca at least once in their life; they give charity to the poor, especially during their holy month of Ramadan; they do not eat during the daytime in the month of Ramadan; and they say the *shahadah*, which reminds them that there is no god but Allah and that Muhammad is his prophet. In fact, the way you become a Muslim is to say this in front of two Muslims who are listening to you: "There is no god but God, and Muhammad is the messenger of God." This is the shahadah, and it is the most important sentence in all of Islam.

Muhammad is at the center of Islam but not in the way that Jesus is at the center of Christianity. Christians believe Jesus was God, but Muslims believe Muhammad was a prophet of God, a human being. Muhammad (not, as it's often spelled, Mohammed) lived about 1,400 years ago. Whenever Muslims say the name of the prophet Muhammad, they always say "peace be upon him." It is a way of showing respect.

Muhammad was not just a good prophet, he was also a good general. He helped to start the Islamic Empire, which was the biggest empire that ever was and ever would be. The Islamic Empire began in Arabia with Muhammad, but a hundred years after his death it stretched from France to India!

Islam spread to Persia and to Turkey in the north. It spread to Afghanistan, and Tajikistan, and Uzbekistan, and Pakistan (in fact, if a country has a name that ends in *stan*, you can bet it's Muslim). Islam spread to India in the east and to Africa in the south. It spread to Indonesia, Sumatra, Brunei, Malaya, Java, the southern Philippine islands, parts of Thailand and Cambodia and Singapore, and parts of the little islands of the South Seas, like Fiji.

There are even Muslims in places you might never think had any Muslims. There are millions of Muslims in China. There is a fairly big (and fairly cold) group of Muslims in Finland. The

Muslims in Bosnia who are having such a hard time now have been living there for over 500 years.

Most of the people who have become Muslims did so because they believe in Islam and not because they were conquered by Muslim armies and forced to convert. Today, Islam is the fastest-growing religion in the United States.

Even though Jews and Muslims have been fighting over Israel for the past fifty years, Jews and Muslims lived together in peace for hundreds of years. The time Jews lived under Muslim rule some 800 years ago is called by Jews "The Golden Age of Judaism" because the Muslims were so good to the Jews in their lands. The Muslim Vizier Al-Kadi al Fadil and later the Caliph Al Fadal had a Jewish doctor and friend named Maimonides, who was the most important Jewish thinker of medieval times. (Viziers and caliphs are up there right under sultan as the highest people in the Islamic Empire.)

Muslims did make enemies, and they did fight lots of wars, because not every country they conquered wanted to stay conquered, even by nice Muslims. Muslims and Christians fought in Israel during the Crusades about 700 years ago. And about 200 years ago Muslims and Hindus were fighting in India. Pakistan was cut out of India in 1947 and made a separate country because the Hindus and Muslims could not get along. Having an empire and having a religion are hard to do together. Having the empire usually makes your people forget the teachings of your religion, because conquering people and loving people just don't go together, and loving people is what most religions are really all about. Christianity and Islam both found that out after they tried to have kind empires and it didn't work out.

Muslims teach that Abraham was their ancestor too. Abraham and his wife Sarah had a son named Isaac. Isaac is the ancestor of the Jews. Abraham and his other wife, Hagar, had a son named

Ishmael. Ishmael is the ancestor of the Arab Muslims and the prophet Muhammad. This means that Jews and Muslims are kind of cousins. It would be good for peace in the Middle East if Jews and Muslims would always remember that!

The cities of Mecca and Medina are very holy cities for Muslims. Every Muslim is supposed to make a pilgrimage to Mecca at least once. A pilgrimage is a trip you make, not to see a beach or Disneyland, but to see a holy place.

There are about a billion Muslims living in the world today, and about 5 million of them live in America. Most people think that all Muslims are Arabs, but the truth is most Arabs are Muslims, but most Muslims are not Arabs. Out of every five Muslims, only about one of them is an Arab.

What makes us very sad is that some people only hear about Islam or Muslims when they hear about some bombing or plane hijacking done by crazy people who happen to be Muslims. This makes some people afraid of Islam and Muslims, and this fear is just plain wrong! Muslims are taught by Islam to be good people. They have lots of good rules about how to behave. Good Muslims don't smoke, and they don't drink alcohol.

Muslims have many good rules, and none of those rules teach that it is okay for Muslims to go around killing folks. Muslims who hurt people are not doing a Muslim thing! Muslims who hurt people are doing a bad thing that is against the teachings of Islam. There are nuts in every religion (we know because lots of them come to talk to us!), but the religion did not teach these folks to be nuts. They came that way.

CHAPTER 6

Who Are
the Big Teachers?

All religions have teachers, but some religions have one really big teacher. The religions that anybody can join are the religions that have one big teacher, and the religions that come from tribes that you have to be born into hardly ever have one big teacher. Judaism and Hinduism have great teachers like Moses and Krishna, but Judaism and Hinduism are religions that come more from the teachings of a tribe than from the teachings of one big teacher. On the other hand, Buddhism, Christianity, and Islam are three big open religions in the world that are *built* on the teachings of one big teacher. Gautama Buddha, Jesus Christ, and the prophet Muhammad did not just help Buddhism, Christianity, and Islam, they made them. Here are their stories.

Buddha

The Buddha said he was a guide, not a god, but sometimes people get confused about this because of the way Buddhists pray in front of statues of the Buddha. Buddhists believe that when the Buddha was born, blind people could see, lame people could walk, the tigers stopped growling, and the whole world was sunny. Now do you understand why it's hard to believe that the Buddha was just a guide?

Buddhists treat the Buddha like a god even though in Buddhism, as we said already, there are no gods, just teachings. Some of the Buddhist prayer places, called *temples* or *pagodas,* have relics of the Buddha. A relic is a piece of a holy person's body that people treat in a special way, put in a special place, and say prayers in front of because they want to be close to the holy person. One pagoda in Sri Lanka has what they say is a tooth from the Buddha. (Of course he had no cavities!) They call it "the Temple of the Sacred Tooth." In Yangon, Myanmar (which used to be called Rangoon, Burma), there is a pagoda with some of the Buddha's hair, though this is kind of confusing because in most of the statues the Buddha is bald.

You see statues of the Buddha all over the world. When you learn about these statues, you can tell where they come from just by looking at their shape. In southeast Asia and India, most of the Buddha statues are fat and round. In China they are long and skinny, and in Japan lots of Buddha statues have pointy shoulder pads, but they are all Buddha statues, and they all show the love and respect that Buddhists have for this great teacher of wisdom.

Buddha's name was not Buddha any more than Jesus' last name was Christ. Buddha and Christ aren't names, they're titles, like general, president, king. Buddha means "the one who is awake" or "the one who knows." Buddha's real name was Siddhartha Gautama of the Sakyas. Siddhartha was born in the mountains of Nepal, north of India. His father was a king and was really rich. His mother was a queen (which usually happens when your father is a king). He remembered wearing silk clothes and having servants hold umbrellas over him to keep him out of the sun or the rain. Even his elephants had silver saddles!

When he was sixteen years old, Siddhartha married a neighboring princess whose name was Yasodhara. Siddhartha Gautama and Yasodhara had a son named Rahula. Everything was going great for Siddhartha until he was in his twenties. Then he kind of freaked out.

Siddhartha suddenly realized that all the fancy stuff around him did not make him happy. His father got worried that Siddhartha was about to leave home, go wandering around, and give up being a prince. To stop this, Siddhartha's father bought him even more wonderful things to enjoy and built him palaces to live in. The king even ordered that no sick people, no old people, no poor people should be allowed anywhere near his son. He wanted his son to see only beautiful, happy, healthy people all the time, but no matter what his father did, nothing helped to cheer up Siddhartha.

The "Legend of the Four Sights," the most famous Buddhist story, tells us what happened next. One day when Siddhartha was taking a walk, he came across an old man with a gray beard and no teeth, bent over and leaning on a walking stick. That day Siddhartha learned about old age. The next day on his walk, Siddhartha saw a sick man lying by the side of the road, and so he learned that the world was also filled with sickness. On a third walk, Siddhartha saw a dead person for the first time in his life, and so he learned about death. On the fourth walk, Siddhartha saw a monk. Because such people had decided to own nothing but a bowl and live with hardly any stuff, the monk's head was shaved, and he wore a brown robe and held a begging bowl. On that day Siddhartha learned about giving up all the things of the world. This is what he learned from these four sights: *The world is full of sickness, old age, and death!* This is the question he asked: *Where is the world where there is no sickness, no old age, and no death?*

The rest of his life was spent trying to find that world where nobody got sick, where nobody got old, and where nobody died. Then one night when he was just twenty-nine years old, Siddhartha mounted his great white horse and rode away to the edge of the forest. There he gave the horse to a servant to take it back to the palace, and to tell his wife and son that he had gone off to find *enlightenment*, which means he had gone off to figure out what really mattered and what was stupid.

Siddhartha spent six years wandering around the forest with his head shaved, wearing just rags for clothes. During the first part of his time in the forest, Siddhartha found some Hindu teachers called *Yogis* to teach him all about Hinduism. In the end, Siddhartha decided that these Yogis were still too tied down to all the stuff of the earth and to all the millions of gods they worshiped. So he left them.

He did not find enlightenment with the Hindus.

The next stage of his journey took him to some people called *ascetics,* who were really into not eating and doing everything to get your body so weak that your mind could get clear about things. Siddhartha learned to live on six grains of rice a day and got so skinny he could feel his spine by pressing in on his stomach. He almost died by not eating anything, but he was saved and decided that six grains of rice a day was just silly, because it just made him hungry and weak rather than wise.

He did not find enlightenment with the ascetics.

One night in the month of May, Siddhartha was in the town of Gaya in the northeast part of India and was sitting completely still while meditating under a peepul tree.

Seeing that Siddhartha was getting close to being enlightened, the evil god Mara tried to get him to move, breaking his attention to his meditation, by bringing him beautiful women and playing some great tunes. This did not work. Siddhartha did not boogie. Then the evil god tried to scare Siddhartha into moving, but he did not move, and he was not scared. All the swords and arrows Mara fired at Siddhartha to kill him just turned into flower petals before they touched him. Siddhartha touched the earth with his finger, and it began to thunder and the earth roared, and Mara took a hike.

The peepul tree (which lots of Buddhists call the Bo tree) sent out flowers of red. Then—*wham!*—it happened! Siddhartha got enlightened! Siddhartha became the Buddha. He saw the way the universe really was, and he understood everything. Then Mara the evil one returned and laughed at the Buddha. Mara said something like: "Congratulations! You have enlightenment now! Big deal! Let me tell you something: What you know now is so hard to understand, what you know now is so big, what you know now is so deep, *nobody* in the whole wide world will ever be able to understand it. You might as well disappear right now because there will be nobody for you to talk to *ever!*"

This was the first thing that Mara had ever said that bothered the Buddha, but being a Buddha, he thought for a while and then just looked at Mara and said, "There will always be some who will understand."

Jesus

Christians believe that Jesus was God, but Christians also believe that Jesus was a Jewish carpenter. These two sides of Jesus are what makes his life both very important and very hard to understand. In the first three or four hundred years, Christians argued a lot about whether Jesus was mostly God or mostly human or equal parts of both. What is important is that Jesus was not like any other person who ever lived.

Jesus the human being lived only thirty-three years and was killed by the Romans. He was killed because too many people loved him and too many people were following him. People not only loved Jesus, they believed that he was the Messiah. The Messiah is the person sent by God to fix all the bad stuff in the world and make peace on earth and get rid of sin.

Sin is turning away from God. Sin is the bad things we do. All Jews and Christians and Muslims believe that. Christians also believe that the first sin was the bad thing Adam and Eve did in the Garden of Eden. God told Adam not to eat the fruit of a certain tree in the Garden of Eden but Adam (and Eve) ate it anyway. Because of this sin, Adam and Eve were kicked out of the Garden. Christians believe that this sin was so huge, it touched the lives of all people who would ever live. The death and coming back to life of Jesus, Christians believe, wiped away the sin of Adam and gave hope to people that God was very close again.

The coming back to life of Jesus after the Romans killed him by nailing his body to a cross has a big name, *Resurrection.* Christians believe that Jesus was resurrected after being dead for three days. Jesus was killed on a Friday and buried the same day in a cave with a big rock in front of it. On Sunday the rock was rolled away from the opening of the cave, and the body of Jesus was gone.

After that, the followers of Jesus saw him for forty days in different places and at different times. People like Mary Magdalene saw him. Two friends of Jesus saw him on a journey to the town of Emmaus. The Apostles, Jesus' closest friends, saw him. The Apostles were: Peter, James, John, Andrew, Matthew, Thomas, Philip, Bartholomew, Simon, Thaddaeus, and another

James who was the son of Alphaeus. (Judas, who betrayed Jesus, was replaced by Matthias.) The Apostles were the last people to see Jesus before he went back to heaven.

Jesus was born to Joseph and Mary. Before he was born, an angel named Gabriel (the same angel Muslims believe gave the Quran to Muhammad later on) came to Mary and told her that she would have a baby boy named Jesus, and that he would not come from Joseph but from God. Joseph knew that this was a big miracle, and he took good care of Mary and Jesus.

When it was time for Mary to give birth, Joseph and Mary were traveling to the city of Bethlehem. There was no room at the inn (and all the hotels and motels were booked solid), and so Jesus had to be born in a manger. Some shepherds came to visit, along with three wise men who brought birthday gifts to the baby Jesus. They gave him gold, frankincense, and myrrh. A beautiful star also rose in the sky the night Jesus was born.

There are not many stories about Jesus' childhood, but you can bet that Mary and Joseph never had to ask him a million times to clean up his room or take out the garbage! There is a story that when he was twelve, his parents traveled with him to Jerusalem because it was time for the holiday of Passover. They lost Jesus for a while because Mary thought Joseph had him and Joseph thought that Mary had him. When they found him, he was in the Temple listening to the priests and asking them questions. Everyone who talked to him knew right away that this was a boy who was very close to God.

Jesus taught everywhere. He taught in the synagogues, in the fields, on the hills. One of his most important teachings was the Sermon on the Mount, which Jesus taught on a hill in the Galilee, which is in the northern part of Israel. There Jesus taught that poor people were just as close to God as rich people (closer even!). He taught that we should not toot our own horn but be very quiet and modest and humble. He taught that we should help everyone who needs help. He taught people to make peace. He taught people to cut other people some slack. He taught people to care about what was fair and what was right. He taught people to do things for good reasons, and most of all he taught people never ever to give up, because even if things did not work out here on earth, they would work out just fine in heaven.

Jesus told great stories, called *parables*. Parables are not only good stories, they are stories that teach us how to live and how to do the right thing. Here are some of the best parables of Jesus:

- He told the story of a father who had a son who was a jerk, but the father never gave up on his son and helped him to be a good person. This story teaches us never to give up on our family.
- He told a story about a shepherd who went to look for one lost sheep even though all the other sheep were okay. This story teaches us to never give up on anyone because God never gives up on us.
- He told a story about a good Samaritan. The people Jesus was talking to thought Samaritans were bad, but Jesus said that this Samaritan was a good person who stopped to help somebody even though he did not have to. This story teaches us to help people who need help.
- He told a story about a small mustard seed that grew into a big tree. This story teaches us that faith that starts out small can get very big if we just let it grow.

Each of these stories helped his followers learn the lessons of living a good life.

When Jesus was about thirty years old, he came to his cousin

John, who was usually called John the Baptist. Jesus walked into the water and asked John to baptize him like all the other people. Then the sky opened up and the Spirit of God came down and said to everybody there at the river, "This is my beloved Son in whom I am well pleased."

This was more than enough to convince John and everybody there that Jesus was not a person like everyone else. That is when he first knew that God had made him special. That was when Jesus understood that he had special work from God to do. Like the Buddha and Moses, who wandered in the desert to get strong and pure before they started their work, Jesus went into the desert for forty days of praying and not eating. Then he came back to the world ready to do what God wanted, just the way God wanted it done.

For the next three years, Jesus taught and did miracles and showed people that God is love. His followers said that Jesus was the Messiah, and this got Jewish leaders very angry. Judaism taught that the Messiah would have to bring peace everywhere, and since Jesus didn't do that, they could not believe that he was the Messiah. Jesus also said that the Temple in Jerusalem would be destroyed, and the Jewish priests who worked in the Temple got angry at Jesus for saying that.

What got the Roman leaders angry at Jesus was that he was causing trouble for them everywhere. He taught his followers not to go into the army and kill people. He criticized rich people and said that poor people had a much better chance of getting into heaven. He taught that the kingdom of Rome was not going to last forever, but that the Kingdom of God would last forever. Even though Jesus made followers everywhere, Jesus also made enemies everywhere, and his enemies were very powerful. They wanted him dead. With all the powerful enemies he made, it is no wonder that they got him arrested and that they got him killed.

The death of Jesus is a very touchy point between some Jews and some Christians. The problem is that as time passed, the story of the death of Jesus got blamed on the Jews alone. This happened because Christianity became the religion of the Roman Empire in the year 325. This made blaming the Romans for the death of Jesus very hard, and it made blaming the Jews very easy.

What happened next was very sad. Over the years, many Christian children were brought up believing that the Jews killed Jesus. Hating Jews for killing Jesus got into the thinking of some Christians in a very deep way. It is kind of like the way that the idea that blacks are not as good as whites got into the thinking of some white people. Bad ideas can sink in just as deeply as good ideas.

When the Holocaust came, many millions of Jews were killed, and then things started to change. Many Christians began to understand that it was wrong to blame Jews for the death of Jesus. Christians began to realize that Jesus had taught people to love. They began to understand that teaching people to hate Jews had helped to make the Holocaust happen.

Jesus is by far the most followed leader and teacher in any religion anywhere and anytime. Christians believe that Jesus will come back to the earth a second time to finish all the work he didn't have a chance to finish the first time. Everybody who is a Christian is really waiting for the Second Coming of Jesus.

Muhammad

Muhammad was a prophet. Muslims believe that he was the last prophet, the last messenger from God. This means that Muhammad was not a god or a god-man. Muslims do not think about Muhammad the way Buddhists think about Buddha or Christians think about Jesus. Muhammad is much more like Moses and the other prophets in the Hebrew Bible. He was a human being who got a special message from God and gave it to the world. Muslims teach that he was a perfect human being but that he was just a person, not a god.

Muhammad was born in Mecca 1,425 years ago. His father, whose name was Abdullah, died before he was born, and his mother, Amina, died before he was six years old. First his grandfather Abdul Muttalib and then his uncle Abu Talib cared for him as a boy and protected him. Muhammad lived in the desert with the Bedouin Arabs. He was respected and trusted by everybody, and they called him *al-amin*, "the trusted one."

When he was twenty-five, Muhammad married a rich widow who was fifteen years older than he. Her name was Khadijah. She put him in charge of her caravans, which went to Syria. This job gave him time to think more and more about God. People who liked to think about God were called in Arabic *hanifs*.

Like Moses and Jesus, Muhammad saw God in the desert after going there alone. He was in a cave on Mount Hira, which is near the city of Mecca, when the angel Gabriel came to him and told him, "Read!" Muhammad told the angel that he did not know how to read. The angel asked him again and again.

Muhammad was afraid of being called by the angel, but his wife, Khadijah, calmed him down. She told him that he was a good man and would make a great prophet, and he should do what Allah wanted him to do because Allah would help him.

This happens a lot with prophets. Moses was afraid and did not want to go when God called him. Maybe one of the ways you get the job of prophet is by not wanting it. Another thing that is true of most prophets is that things usually start out badly. Soon after Muhammad was called to be a prophet of God, his wife and uncle died. Then the people who believed he was a prophet got beaten up. His message was that people should not bow down to idols, which were little statues of gods. He taught that there is just one true God and that it is forbidden to make a statue or picture of God. This got the idol worshipers and the idol makers very angry. For the next ten years things were awful.

Muhammad moved to a little town called Medina, which is north of Mecca. Originally the name of the place was Yathrib, but because Muhammad lived there, it later was called in Arabic Madinat al-Nabi, which means "the city of the prophet." It is also called Madinat al-Rasul, which means "the city of the messenger." Those names were pretty long, so the town was called Medina for short. The trip on which Muhammad moved from Mecca to Medina was called the *hijrah*. Muslims count that year as year one of the way they count time.

In Medina, Muhammad found more and more people who believed he was the prophet of Allah. He had to fight armies from Mecca. He won, even though his army was much smaller than the armies he was fighting. He kept on winning until the whole Arabian peninsula was a Muslim area. Even when things started to go well for Muhammad, he still lived a very simple life. He lived in a small house made of clay, milked his own goats, and wore a simple coat of cheap cloth.

Muhammad got messages from the angel Gabriel for twenty-three years, until his death. One night he was taken by the angel Gabriel to Jerusalem, and from Jerusalem, Muhammad was taken to heaven on his horse al-Barak. This going to heaven showed to all his followers that he was the most special prophet from God.

Just before he died, Muhammad returned to Mecca. This trip

to Mecca by Muhammad is imitated by all Muslims. It is called the *hajj*. If you are a Muslim who has made a pilgrimage to Mecca, you have your name changed. You add *al haj* in front of your name to show people with pride that you have been to Mecca. It is a sign of pride and honor and love.

Muhammad taught that people needed to give themselves to God all the way! Muhammad taught that everything belongs to God, and we must be God's perfect servants. Giving ourselves to God all the way meant many things to Muhammad. It meant following the law of God, which was in the Quran. This law is called *al-shariah*, which means "the path." (Judaism calls the law of God the *halacha*, which also means "the path.")

The basic idea of the law is that it is a way to say thank you to God. Muslims believe that God owns everything, and we owe God everything. Islam is the way Muslims say thank you to God and pay God back for all the blessings God has given to us. In the Quran we learn, "God is the rich one and we are the poor ones." (XLVII, 38)

Muhammad also taught Muslims that the community of all the Muslims in the world is very important and that Muslims should stick together. The community of all the Muslims in the world is called in Arabic the *umma*. Helping the umma and being a close part of the umma is very important to Muslims because of the teachings of Muhammad. He also taught that people of any color from any place should be welcomed into Islam. Racism is against the teachings of Muhammad, and that is why Muslims come in all colors and from every place.

Muhammad died in the city of Medina 1,363 years ago. Muslims say "peace be upon him" after saying the name of Muhammad. To have a billion people say your name with love every day is not a small thing.

CHAPTER 7

What Are
the Holy Books?

The holy books of the religions of the world do two things. First, the holy books tell us what the great teachers learned about God. This is important because the great ones knew more about God than we do, and we need their wisdom. The second thing the holy books do is let us look at God through them. Holy books are like eyeglasses that help us to see things in the world that we would not see without them. When we see people without the holy books, we just see people, but when we see people through those books, we see that all people are special and all people deserve our love and respect.

Holy books are important, but not all holy books teach the same things. You have to read all of them and compare them to figure out what is the same and what isn't. Here are some of the holy books that billions of people have used for thousands of years to learn about God, the world, and each other.

The Vedas

The holy books of the Hindus are written in a language called Sanskrit. Sanskrit comes from an old language called Vedic, which came from the land called Persia (today we call it Iran). Around six thousand years ago the Vedic people invaded India and brought with them their language and their stories. The stories are about many gods, and these stories became the first and most important holy books of Hinduism. Most of the stories are written like poems or songs, and this is because it is easier to remember a song than just words. The oldest Hindu songs are called the Rig-Veda, the Sama-Veda, the Yajur-Veda, and the Atharva-Veda. These are the oldest Hindu holy books.

Each of these books were divided into *samhitas*, which were songs to be sung while meditating or praying; *brahmanas*, which were the parts of the books the Hindu priests were supposed to read; and *arinyakas*, which were stories from the people who lived in the forests. The most important part of each book is the last part, which is called the Upanishad. The Upanishads were the parts with the deep teachings and the most wisdom.

All these books together are called the Veda. This is just like the Bible, which has many parts and one name for all of them together. Hindus have a neat way of teaching the Vedas: They sing them. They also teach their children to sing them, because they know that it is easier to remember a song than a lesson. For those folks who want to know just the main ideas of the Veda, there is a book called the Brahmasutra.

The Vedas are not the only Hindu holy books; they are just the oldest. Two other very important works for Hinduism are the Ramayana and the Mahabharata. The Ramayana is about the god Rama and his birth, childhood, and adventures. The Mahabharata tells the story of a family called the Kauravas, who were being attacked, but everything came out all right because of the help of the god Krishna. Both of these stories are supposed to help people learn the difference between right and wrong.

The most important holy book in Hinduism today is the Bhagavad-Gita, which means "the song of the Lord." It is a part of the Mahabharata story. The Gita is a story of the conversation between the hero Arjuna and the god Krishna, who had taken human form to drive Arjuna's chariot. Arjuna is going into the battle of Kurukshetra (say that ten times with potato chips in your mouth!), and he is worried that he will have to kill people in the battle. Krishna tells him that he is in the warrior caste and so he must fight the battle. The Gita is much more than a story about battles. It is a story of how to gain *moksha*, which is getting free from all the things of this world.

The Hebrew Bible

Again, some people call this the Old Testament, but the Jews who love these books don't think of them as "old," so the best way to name these holy books is the Hebrew Bible.

The Hebrew Bible has three main parts. The first part is called the Torah. The Torah has five different books in it: Genesis, Exodus, Leviticus, Numbers, and Deuteronomy. If you go into any synagogue, you will find that these five books of the Torah are written on a scroll made of sheepskin and connected to two wooden posts. The whole scroll is way over a hundred feet long, so it is kept rolled up on two posts. To make one Torah scroll, you either have to sew together lots of sheepskins or else you have to find one humongous sheep.

The Torah is written in Hebrew, and Hebrew is written from right to left, the opposite of English. The words of the Torah scroll are written in black ink made of blackberries, and a quill pen is used to write the letters onto the sheepskin, which is colored white to make the black letters stand out.

The Torah is written—really it is copied, since nobody is allowed to add any new words to the Torah—by a special Torah copier who is called a *sofer*. Being a sofer is a good job because you are always writing holy words, but it is a hard job because all your work has to be *perfect*.

Jews read all five books of the Torah, a little each week, at Saturday, Monday, and Thursday prayer services, so that by the end of one year they have read every word of all five books of the Torah.

This is what's in the Torah: The book of Genesis (*beresheet* in Hebrew) is about how God made everything and then made the first people, and then things got crummy and God flooded the whole world but saved Noah and two of each animal, plus the bugs. Then came Abraham and Sarah, their son Isaac, and Isaac's wife, Rebekah, who had twins, Jacob and Esau. One of Jacob's thirteen children was Joseph, who got a coat of many colors from his father. This ticked off his brothers, who sold him as a slave in Egypt. But Joseph made a big success of himself there, and at the end of Genesis, he helps save his family from a famine.

The book of Exodus (*shmot* in Hebrew) starts with Moses, who grew up as a prince in the house of the pharaoh, even though he was Jewish. Moses used some big-time miracles from God to get the Jewish people out of Egypt, like bringing lots of flies and opening up a path of dry land through the Red Sea. Moses then took the people to Mount Sinai, where God gave Moses the Ten Commandments and other laws and teachings.

The book of Leviticus (*vayikra* in Hebrew), the third book of the Torah, has some parts that are great and some parts that are, frankly, pretty boring. Leviticus has the teaching that we should love our neighbor like we love ourselves. It has lots of laws

teaching us to feed the hungry and lift up those folks who have to sleep in the dust, but Leviticus also has old laws about sacrifices that are kind of gross. Sacrifices were things people brought to the holy places to thank God and to feed the priests. Some of the sacrifices were little meal cakes, some were pigeons, and some were even cows and goats.

Leviticus also has the laws that many Jews still follow about what you can eat (kosher food) and what you can't. Here's how the kosher laws work: An animal must chew its cud and have split hooves to be kosher. Cud, if you must know, is animal vomit, which is eaten again because it wasn't digested the first time! Pigs have split hooves, but they don't chew their cud so they are not kosher.

The word *kosher* means "fit," or "okay by God." Muslims keep kosher too (no Muslim can eat pork), but they call it *hallal.* For a fish to be kosher, it must have fins and scales. Perch are in, shrimp are out. For a bird to be kosher it must not be a bird of prey. That means that if a bird eats other birds or fish, it is not kosher. Chickens and turkeys are okay, but vultures are not. This is a relief, because who would want to eat vulture soup with matzoh balls when sick?

The book of Numbers (*bamidbar* in Hebrew) is the fourth book of the Torah, and like Leviticus, it also has some interesting and some boring stuff. Numbers has a great blessing in it, one that is very simple and very beautiful: "May the Lord bless you and keep you; may the Lord's face shine upon you and be kind to you; may God watch over you always and grant you peace." What a great blessing! The boring stuff is about the priests, because there are no priests in Judaism anymore.

The book of Deuteronomy (*devarim* in Hebrew) is the last book of the Torah, and it is kind of like a review of the stories and the laws that came before. Deuteronomy even puts in another copy of the Ten Commandments just so nobody will forget them. The book ends with the death of Moses, who has brought the people to the land of Israel after forty years of walking around the desert.

The second part of the Hebrew Bible is called the Prophets (*neviim* in Hebrew). Prophets were the special teachers who talked to God, and this part of the Bible is the teachings of the prophets who came after Moses. The main prophets who got books named after them were: Joshua, Samuel, Isaiah, Jeremiah, Ezekiel, Hosea, Joel, Amos, Obadiah, Jonah, Micah, Nahum, Habakkuk, Zephaniah, Haggai, Zechariah, and Malachi. There are also some history books, like Kings (I and II) and Judges, in this part of the Bible, and these tell what happened after Moses died.

The third part of the Hebrew Bible is called the Writings (*ketuvim* in Hebrew). This part has lots of different kinds of books in it. There are some prophet books, like Daniel, Ezra, and Nehemiah. There are some history books, like Chronicles (I and II). There are two books that tell the stories of women who were very brave. They are the book of Ruth and the book of Esther. There is a book of beautiful love poems called the Song of Songs. There is the book of Proverbs, which is filled with short, wise sayings to help us get through the day. The book of Ecclesiastes is by King Solomon, who was rich but bored. This story reminds us of what the Buddha went through in his life. The book of Job is the story of a good man who is tested by God to see if he would turn against God if God took away all his stuff. God did, and Job didn't. And there is the book of Lamentations, which is a book of real sadness about the way the Temple in Jerusalem was destroyed by the Babylonians.

The most famous part of the Writings are the 150 psalms. The psalms are like poems for God. They are very beautiful, and they help us to learn what it feels like to love God. They help us to remember that we can talk to God when we are happy or angry, lonely or scared. God is always there for us. The most famous psalm is number 23. You probably remember it. If you don't, we put it in on pages 196–197.

The New Testament

There are twenty-seven books that make up the New Testament, but there are really only four *kinds* of books.

The first kind of book you will find in the New Testament is called a Gospel. The Gospels were written in Greek, but the word *gospel* comes from two old German words that mean "good news," and that's because the stories about Jesus are real good news for all Christians everywhere. In Greek, the Gospels were called *evangelion,* which also means "good news." There are four Gospels in the New Testament, and they are called Matthew, Mark, Luke, and John. The Gospels tell the story of the life and teachings of Jesus and the story of how he died. The Gospels also tell the most important part of the story, which is the part where Jesus rose from the dead after being dead for three days.

The story of what happened to the followers of Jesus after he died and rose from the dead is in the book called The Acts of the Apostles. The Acts of the Apostles is the second kind of book in the New Testament. This book tells the story of how two guys, Peter and Paul, did so much work to spread the teachings of Jesus. It also tells us about how the first Christians shared everything with each other.

The third kind of book in the New Testament is called an epistle. Epistles are letters, and there are twenty-one of them. Some epistles are long, some are short. It just depended on what the writer of the epistle had to say and how much paper he had that day. There is a letter from James, two from Peter, three from John, one from Jude, and one to the Hebrews. We don't know for sure who wrote some of the letters, but the oldest and most important letters came from Paul. Paul wrote letters to the Romans, the Corinthians (two letters), the Galatians, the Ephesians, the Philippians, the Colossians, the Thessalonians (two letters), to Timothy (two letters), to Titus, and to Philemon. Not everybody wrote back to Paul after he wrote to them, but he was a good man and didn't mind.

The fourth part of the New Testament is a book called Revelation. The book of Revelation is filled with stories of strange dreams, intense battles, numbers that have hidden meanings, dragons, earthquakes, and secret signs of the future. The book of Revelation tells about how Jesus is going to return to earth and fight a huge and bloody war against the bad folks in the world and also against the dragons. You really have to know all the bad things that were happening to Christians at the time to understand all the signs of this weird book, but what it all means is that you can *always* trust God to be with you.

The Quran

Sometimes this holy book of Islam is spelled *Koran*, but Quran is closer to the way it is pronounced in Arabic, which is the language it was written in. The word *Qur'an* comes from the Arabic word *kara*, which means "to read or recite something."

The whole Quran (which is shorter than the Hebrew Bible and about the same length as the New Testament) has 114 chapters, called *suras*. The suras are divided into two big parts. First are those suras that happened before the prophet Muhammad made a pilgrimage to Mecca, and the second part are those that happened after he made the pilgrimage. Muslims believe that the whole Quran was taught to Muhammad by the angel Gabriel, who read it from a big stone in heaven, the *lawh al-mahfuz*, where every word of it is written in the stone.

Some of the suras are long, and some are just two or three verses. The suras are not songs, like the Vedas, and they are not prose, like most of the New Testament. The suras are sort of like poems. They have a rhythm when you read them in Arabic, and they are very beautiful. Some of the suras are about people who are in the Hebrew Bible: Abraham, Hagar, Ishmael, Jethro, and Joseph are just a few of them.

The message of the Quran is that God, Allah, is one, that God created the world and people, and that God wants people to do what God says. The people who do what God wants will go to heaven and the ones who don't will go to hell.

The whole Quran is read in sections over the course of a year by Muslims, just like the Torah is read over a year by Jews. There are little notes in the Quran that tell you what parts to read every day, every week, and every month. Muslims kiss the Quran, just as Jews kiss the Torah. They carry copies of the Quran with them, and they have to prepare themselves and wash themselves before they will open it up and read from it.

CHAPTER 8

Where Are the Holy Places?

From the very beginning of religions, many people believed that God had favorite places. If you wanted to find God, you would go to God's favorite place and look around. Some of the places where it was easier to find God were on a hilltop or in a cave, in tall trees or on big rocks, near rivers or lakes, or in valleys or fields. But lots of times the place people thought it was easiest to find God was on a mountain. Sometimes special buildings were put up near the special places.

The teaching that there are holy places where God is very close is hard for many folks to understand. After all, if God is everywhere, how can you be closer to God in just one special place? To understand holy places, it helps to think of graves. When somebody you loved dies and you bury them in the ground, the place where you buried the person becomes a holy place. The memory of the person who died is with you wherever you go, but when you are at the person's grave, the memories are stronger and, in a strange way, that person is closer to you. A holy place for a religion is a place where God seems closer.

Here are some of the places people over thousands of years have believed are holy places, the places where God is very close.

Mecca and Medina

Two cities in the west of Arabia are the holiest places for Muslims. They are the cities where Muhammad got the teaching from God that made Islam a religion. The two cities have one name for both of them together. They are called the *Haramain*, which means "the two holy places." Medina is about 180 miles north of Mecca in the desert of Saudi Arabia. Medina was the home town of Muhammad. When he died and was buried in Medina, many Muslims came to visit his grave.

Mecca is a town about 50 miles from the Red Sea in the Arabian desert, and it is even more holy for Muslims than Medina. Many Muslims want to be buried in Mecca when they die, because they believe that even the earth of that city is special and holy. In fact, when Muslims pray anywhere in the world, they first find out what direction Mecca is in, and then they face that way when they pray.

The most holy place in the holy city of Mecca is called the Kabah. The Kabah is a building that was in Mecca way before Muhammad was born. It is about 36 feet long and 30 feet wide and 18 feet high. Muslims believe that Adam, the same Adam who is in the Hebrew Bible, built the Kabah and that Abraham and his son Ishmael fixed it up. Muslims believe that Ishmael and his mother, Hagar, are buried under the Kabah.

The Kabah today is covered in black silk and wool, and around it is a band of words from the Quran. The covering is called in Arabic the *kiswa*. It is replaced with a new kiswa every year at the time when Muslims from all over the world come to visit Mecca on a special holy visit called a *hajj*. Every Muslim is supposed to make a pilgrimage to Mecca at least once in his life. They come to the Kabah in Mecca, and they walk around it seven times. Millions of Muslims come to Mecca every year for the pilgrimage.

The inside of the Kabah is a place very few people ever go. You must be a Muslim to enter the Kabah. In fact, you must be a Muslim even to get into the city of Mecca. Inside the Kabah there are marble floors and marble walls and two big stones. On the eastern wall of the inside of the Kabah is a black stone. On the southeastern wall of the Kabah there is another stone, made of granite from Mecca.

Jerusalem

Jerusalem is a holy city for Jews, Christians, and Muslims. For Jews and Christians it is the number one holy place. For Muslims it is the number three holy place, after the cities of Mecca and Medina.

About 3,000 years ago, King David won the city in a war with some folks called the Jebusites. The Bible tells us that King David made Jerusalem the capital of Israel. King David's son Solomon, who was also a king, built a big building in Jerusalem called the Temple. King Solomon built the Temple on a hill called Mount Moriah, the place where the Jews believed God had asked Abraham to sacrifice his son Isaac.

The whole Temple was holy, but there were places in the Temple that were even more holy than other parts. There was a big wall around the Temple, but the bottom of the western wall is all that is left of the Temple today. Jews today still come to this western wall to pray.

A Jewish legend teaches that all the earth is holy, but the Land of Israel is the most holy land on earth. All the cities of the Land of Israel are holy, but Jerusalem is the most holy city. All parts of Jerusalem are holy, but the place where the Temple once stood is the most holy. All parts of the Temple are holy, but the place of the ark that held the Ten Commandments is the most holy place. The whole ark is holy, but the place above the ark and between the two golden angels on the top of the ark is the most holy, because that is where the Spirit of God can be seen. The ark of the covenant in Hebrew is called the *mishkan.* The only people who have ever gotten a good look at the ark were Moses, King David, King Solomon, and maybe Indiana Jones.

Inside the ark were the broken pieces of the first copy of the Ten Commandments, which Moses smashed because he saw the people disobeying the commandments. The place inside the wall, inside the building, inside the room, and inside the golden box was the most holy place in the world for Jews. In fact, when Jews pray to God today, they stand and face in the direction of that place the whole time they are praying.

Jews had real bad luck with the Temple. It got smashed twice. The first time was 2,500 years ago, when it was smashed by Nebuchadnezzar, who was the King of Babylonia (the place called Iraq today). The Temple was rebuilt about seventy years later, but then it got smashed again by the Roman Emperor Titus, who was as mean as Nebuchadnezzar—and that is mean! The only good thing about Titus was that he had a shorter name.

After the Temple was smashed for the second time, it was never rebuilt again, because 1,300 years ago the Muslim Caliph Abdul Malik (a *caliph* is a Muslim emperor) put up a building called the Dome of the Rock (*qubbat al-sakhra*) where the Temple had been. You may have seen it in pictures of Jerusalem. It is the

big beautiful building with a golden dome on top of it. Abdul Malik built it there because of the teaching in the Bible about Abraham being tested by God. The second reason Abdul Malik built the Dome of the Rock on that spot was the teaching in the Quran that the rock where Abraham was tested was also the same rock where the prophet Muhammad went up to heaven.

Another reason the Temple cannot be rebuilt is that Jews teach that only the Messiah can rebuild the Temple when the Messiah comes to make peace in all the world. The Temple Mount, as it is called today, is the holiest place in the holiest city in the world for Jews.

For Christians, the Temple Mount is also very holy, but it is not the holiest place in the city of Jerusalem. There are other holy places in and around the city of Jerusalem, including the places where Jesus was killed and buried, and where he rose from the dead. About 1,600 years ago the emperor Constantine built a church right over the spot where people believed Jesus had been buried. The name of the building is the Church of the Holy Sepulchre (a *sepulchre* is an above-ground grave).

The Ganges River

The Ganges River (called *ganga* in Hindi) is the holiest place for Hindus. It is in India. Hindus believe that the Ganges River begins from the foot of the god Vishnu, flows across the sky as the Milky Way, and comes down to earth through the hair of the god Shiva. The place it comes to earth is in the highest mountains on earth, the Himalayas (where Mount Everest is). From the mountains it flows down into the main part of India.

The two most holy cities on the Ganges River are Hardwar and Banaras. Banaras is by far the most holy city for Hindus. It is called *kasi*, "the city of light." Two other cities on the river,

Prayaga and Allahabad, are also holy cities for Hindus. A holy city is called a *tirthas,* and what makes a city holy is that a god did something special in that city. There are seven holy cities in India.

Hindus make pilgrimages to the holy cities and wash themselves in the holy water of the holy river. Hindus say many prayers when they wash themselves, and even when the water they use comes from somewhere else, they think of that water as coming from the Ganges River.

Many Hindu people who are about to die go to the city of Banaras. Banaras is the city of Shiva, the god of death, so this makes sense. In Banaras, with their families around them, they wait to die. Hindus believe that the god Shiva whispers in the ears of dying people the words that let them die and let them go free. After they are dead, their families burn their bodies into ashes (this practice is called *cremation*) and then scatter their ashes on the Ganges River. In this way the souls of the dead get let loose from the world.

Your Home

You don't have to have a big building with a golden dome or a huge river running through the mountains to have a holy place. Your home is also a holy place. Each religion has a way of showing that a simple home is still a very holy place.

Jews nail a little box to the right side of the doorway leading into a house or a room. Inside the box is a piece of parchment with Hebrew words from the Bible written on it. The box is called a *mezuzah.* Some Jewish homes also have a marker nailed up on the eastern wall of a room, so that they know the direction of Jerusalem. That marker is called a *mizrach.* Muslims have something called a *hamsin* on the doors of their houses. The hamsin is an open hand, which is usually made out of metal and usually has fish hanging from it. The open hand and fish are signs of peace.

Christians will hang up a cross in some or all of the rooms in their house. Sometimes the cross is just a cross, and sometimes the cross also has a little model of Jesus nailed to the cross. A cross with a model of Jesus on it is called a *crucifix.*

Hindus often have carved sculptures of gods, called *arcas,* in their homes. These arcas can be in the house, and gifts are brought for them by the people who live in the house. Buddhists will have statues of different buddhas in their house. These statues are placed where the family can come together to pray.

CHAPTER 9

When Are the Holy Days?

The problem with time is that it just slips away too fast. Before you know it, summer turns into fall, fall turns into winter, then it's spring and summer again. One of the reasons people have religions is that religions help us to hold on to time.

Religions hold on to time in two ways: by making some of the days of the *year* special and by making some of the days of our *lives* special. In this chapter we will look at the special days of the year, and in the next chapter, we will look at the special days of our lives.

The Special Days of the Year

The word *holiday* is really two words, *holy* and *day*, that got mushed together into one word. Holidays are regular days that are made special, made holy, by a religion. Think about it. There is really nothing special about the twenty-fifth day of December. It is just a day at the end of the month of December that comes after the twenty-fourth and before the twenty-sixth, but when December twenty-fifth was made into the holiday of Christmas by Christianity, wow! It sure became a special day for Christians then. The religion of Christianity turned an ordinary day into a holiday, and by doing that it gave all Christians a little piece of time to look forward to, a little piece of time to take out of ordinary time, saying, "This time is special and wonderful and reminds us of good things we forget about on other days."

Now, we all know that there are some holidays that have nothing to do with religion. Some of them are national holidays. For example, the Fourth of July in America is a national holiday, but it is not a religious holiday. It is a day when all Americans celebrate the birthday of America. Memorial Day, Mother's Day, Father's Day, Secretary's Day, Presidents' Day, Be-Kind-to-Animals Day, and National Cheese Dip Day are all like that. They are holidays that don't come from any religion, but they have lots of the values of religions in them. They make us feel closer to our families, closer to our nation . . . and closer to cheese! National holidays are celebrated with parades, fireworks, barbecues, and storewide sales.

Holidays give us a reason to get together with our families and friends, eat a big meal, let the kids run around, and let the adults talk and then fall asleep on the couch. Holidays are a way we hold on to each other. When we sit together and eat together, we can look around and see our family around us. We can see all the ways we are connected to the people in our family. We can thank God that the people in our family who are old are still alive. We can thank God that the people who were sick are getting well, and we can thank God for the babies who have been born into our family. And if people in our family are not well, we can figure out how to try to help them. In a family we all get the strength to carry on with our lives together.

Also, holidays and holiday meals and holiday get-togethers give us a chance to hear the stories of our family. The kids can tell the stories about what they are doing and what they are learning while the adults listen, and the adults can tell the stories of where the family came from while the children listen. They can tell the children what the people were like who are not alive anymore but who were once a part of the family. These stories are the glue that holds families together. Of course, we can tell these stories anytime, but usually we don't. Often we are too busy, so we need holidays to take time to listen to the stories of our lives.

The holidays that come from our religions give us lots of wonderful things to do besides just eating a big meal and falling asleep on the couch. Religious holidays are filled with *rituals,* which are special holy things to do that are very old and come to us from our religion. The rituals of a religious holiday are things that were done on that same holiday by people who lived before us. They are things that will be done by the people who come after us. When Christians go to church on Christmas, they know that what they are doing has been done by Christians for almost two thousand years. Of course some new Christmas things have been added over the years, mainly Christmas trees and Elvis singing "Jingle Bell Rock." But the *most important* part of Christmas is still the same: going to church and thanking God for the birth of Jesus. Knowing this gives Christians a way to hold on to time and each other through the great power of Christmas Day.

The Calendar

Did you ever wonder why some holidays, like Christmas, always happen on the same date each year, but other holidays, like Easter, happen on different dates each year? The answer is that there are two ways to count time. You can count by sun time or you can count by moon time. The moon-time calendar is called the *lunar calendar.* One year of moon time is the time it takes for the moon to get full and shrink down twelve times. The sun-time calendar is called the *solar calendar.* One year of sun time is the time it takes for the earth to revolve around the sun and come back to the same place in its orbit. A year of moon time and a year of sun time are not the same chunk of time. That is the problem.

Twelve months of moon time is 354⅓ days long, and one year of sun time is 365¼ days long. So the sun year is about eleven days longer than the moon year. This means that if you don't *add* some days to the moon-time calendar, it will fall eleven days behind the sun-time year every year. This messes up all the holidays that are supposed to come in a certain season of the year. Try hunting for Easter eggs in the snow!

There are two ways the moon-time people fix this. One way is to add an extra month, called a leap month, to make the calendar fit the seasons again. Jews and Hindus do it this way. Jews add a second spring month called *Adar II* every third, sixth, eighth, eleventh, fourteenth, seventeenth, and nineteenth year of a nineteen-year cycle.

Another way to deal with the difference between sun time and moon time is to do nothing. Muslims do it this way. They do change their moon-time calendar a little. They add one day to the last moon month of the year eleven times in thirty years. This still makes the Muslim months come about ten days earlier each sun-time year.

The holiest month of the Muslim year is called *Ramadan.* It is the ninth month of the Muslim moon-year calendar, when Muslims celebrate how the prophet Muhammad got the holy books of the Quran from the angel Gabriel. Muslims celebrate this holy month by not eating anything during the day. Because the Muslim calendar is not really adjusted to the sun-time calendar, Ramadan gets a little bit earlier each year, and over many years it just kind of travels through the calendar. The Muslims have a beautiful greeting for each other during this time of the year: "May you live to celebrate Ramadan in every season of the year!"

Moon calendars are older than sun calendars. This is because it is easier to count time by the moon than to count time by the sun. The time between one new moon (which is when you can't see the moon at all) to another new moon is about 29 days, 12 hours, 44 minutes, and 3½ seconds . . . about! That is one moon month. After twelve of these moon changes, you get back to the same season you were in when you started to count, and so that is one year.

Counting time by the moon is easy, but counting time by the sun is hard. You have to know just when the longest day is and then wait for one year until it comes again. This is tough. Today we have calendars with all sorts of goofy pictures on them, so counting time is easy for us, but it wasn't always like that. If you had to count time without a calendar, believe us, you would count by moon time. Judaism has always counted time by the moon. So has Hinduism and Buddhism and Islam. Christians count time by the sun, but Christians only count *some* of their holidays that way.

Whatever kind of calendar you use, each holiday has a special message, a special teaching. Most holidays have one of these two messages: The times, they are a-changin', or, Something big happened at this time long ago.

Let's first look at some of the times of the year when religions have holidays to help us see and enjoy and thank God for the way the seasons change and time moves on.

The Change from Summer to Fall

In Judaism there are a lot of holidays in the fall. This is because about 3,000 years ago when the religion we call Judaism got started, most Jews lived as farmers, and so most all the Jewish holidays came after harvest times, when farmers were happy and thankful and had some time for celebrations. The holiday that celebrates the fall harvest is called Sukkot. In fact, Americans have the holiday of Thanksgiving because of Sukkot. The holiday of Sukkot was known by the Pilgrims who came to America, and even though they were Christians, they celebrated Sukkot, which they called the holiday of Tabernacles, because it was in the Bible. The Pilgrims met some Native Americans around Sukkot time and invited them over for a meal of thanksgiving. Fall is full of harvest holidays, and Sukkot and Thanksgiving are just two of them.

Buddhists celebrate a late-summer holiday time that goes from the middle of July to the middle of October. This is the rainy season in southeast Asia and India, where Buddhism began. The holiday called "the Rains Retreat" is a time of heavy study for the Buddhist monks and nuns. There are no parties or weddings or feasts during this time. There is a lot of chanting of the Buddhist stories and a lot of praying for the rain to stop! Hindus also have a rainy-season holiday, which goes from about June to September, in which they worship the god Ganesh.

Because they have a moon-time calendar that they do not adjust each year, Muslims don't have any holidays that come at certain seasons of the year.

The Change from Winter to Spring

Spring is also a big farmers' holiday time, because it is the time for planting things, and it is also the time when cows have calfs, when goats have kids, when sheep have lambs, when ducks have ducklings, when geese have goslings, when owls have owlets. . . . It is the time of the year when almost everything that has babies has babies. Spring is also the time when new green things grow. Spring is the time when the earth seems to be reborn. Religions have always had spring holidays.

In Judaism the spring holiday is Passover. Passover celebrates both the springtime and getting out of Egypt. On Passover, Jews celebrate with a special meal called a *seder.* The seder meal has things in it that celebrate the spring, like parsley and a lamb bone, and also things that celebrate getting out of slavery in Egypt, like the flat bread called *matzoh.* Passover is a great mixture of springtime and freedom time.

In Christianity the spring holiday is Easter. Easter also combines springtime and freedom time. Easter celebrates the death and Resurrection of Jesus. Jesus' being brought back to life after he was killed fits right in with the way the earth is being brought back to life in the springtime. The difference is that what happened to Jesus happened only once, and what happens in the spring happens after every winter. The colored Easter eggs remind us of new life. Eggs are used in many religious rituals to remind us of new life and to bring us hope. Chocolate Easter bunnies do not remind us of anything, but they are so delicious that nobody cares.

The Buddhist springtime holiday is called *Wesak.* Wesak is the day when the Buddha was born. It is also the holiday that celebrates the Buddha becoming a Buddha and the day he died. Wesak comes in the full moon around the month of May.

Wesak is celebrated by hearing long sermons about the life and teachings of the Buddha and with parades around the town and around the Buddhist temples and shrines. (The people usually like the parades more than the sermons.)

The Middle of Winter

The fall and spring holidays usually happen around the time when the day and the night are the same length. These times are called the *equinoxes*. Some holidays happen at the time when the night is as long as it will ever be. This time is called the *winter solstice*. There is also a summer solstice, when the day is as long as it will ever be. There are not too many summer solstice religious holidays. Maybe the reason is that too many people are at the beach then. There is a summer solstice holiday called *Tiragan*, which is celebrated by a religion of people called Zoroastrians, but we did not find any other summer solstice holidays.

There are lots of winter solstice holidays. In the winter, people seem to need religion more than in the summer. Winter is a time when people who live in cold countries are freezing, and most of them are thinking, "When is it going to get warm again?" It is at that time, in the deepest part of winter, that people seem to need some light and some hope. The answer to the winter solstice blahs for Christians is Christmas, and for Jews it is Chanukah.

When Christianity became the religion of the Roman Empire in the year 325, Christmas got put together with the Roman holiday called *Saturnalia*, which was a party-time holiday celebrating the winter solstice. When this happened, Christmas, which was already a happy holiday, got really happy, but the main reason for being happy on Christmas was and is the birth of Jesus, not the new bike under the tree or the eggnog.

The winter holiday of Chanukah remembers the miracle of

Mattathias and his sons, who lived in a town called Modin. They were Jewish fighters trying to get free from the Greeks who ran Israel about 2,060 years ago. They got free, but the Temple in Jerusalem had been wrecked. There was only a little oil left for the big light in the Temple. Then God made the oil burn for eight days—a miracle. In memory of this miracle, Jews light an eight-branched candlestick, called a *menorah*, on Chanukah. Giving gifts on Chanukah was never that big a deal, and other Jewish holidays are way more important in the Jewish year. But when Christmas became a huge gift-giving holiday for Christians, Chanukah became a huge gift-giving holiday for Jews.

The Sabbath

The Sabbath is the invention of Judaism. Christianity and Islam took it into their religions with great joy, but changed the day of the week. The Sabbath for Jews starts on Friday night at sunset and ends on Saturday night at sunset. Muslims take off work Thursday at noon through Friday night, but Muslims don't think of that as their Sabbath. For Muslims, one hour of prayers around noon on Friday, called *al-Jumu'ah*, is the holiest time of the week. For Christians the Sabbath begins at Saturday after 5:00 P.M. and ends Sunday night at sunset.

For Jews and Christians, the Sabbath is the seventh day of the week. It is the day when God rested from making heaven and earth. It is the day God made holy. Now, the neat thing about the Sabbath day is that people were supposed to rest on the Sabbath day, just like God rested. People were supposed to rest and thank God and be with their families. This was a huge idea, because before the idea of the Sabbath came along, people worked all the time. Working all the time is bad for anybody, and God knew this, and that is why God made the Sabbath.

The Beginning of the New Year

Every calendar has a beginning time for the New Year, and every New Year has a holiday with a big family meal. New Year's holidays are a time everybody knows we should thank God for helping to keep us alive for one more year. New Year's Day holidays are kind of like a birthday for everybody.

The Jewish New Year is *Rosh Hashana,* and it happens on the first day of the seventh month of the Jewish moon calendar. Nobody knows why the New Year for Jews doesn't come on the first day of the *first* month, which is in the spring (the seventh month usually comes around September). Rosh Hashana, for Jews, is the birthday of the world. Jews believe it is the day God made the world. The Jewish way to celebrate Rosh Hashana is to go to the synagogue and say prayers and then come home and have a big family meal. Lots of Rosh Hashana foods—like apples, raisins, and prunes—are round and sweet, because of the year coming around again and because it is a happy, sweet time of being together with your family and in your synagogue.

The New Year's festivals in China are also a big deal and a wonderful holiday all over China and everywhere that Chinese Buddhists and Taoists live. The parties and celebrations of the Chinese New Year last for fifteen days. People visit their families, decorate their homes, remember all the wonderful things about their grandmas and grandpas who have died, and go out for a great meal with special dishes prepared just for the New Year. Some people dress up like a dragon and dance in the street while people shoot off firecrackers to scare away evil spirits.

Each Chinese year is named for an animal. There are twelve animals used to name the years: rat, ox, tiger, rabbit, dragon, snake, horse, sheep, monkey, rooster, dog, pig. Each of these animals was supposed to be an animal that blessed the Buddha.

Maybe folks would rather be born in a year of the tiger than a year of the rat, but there's really nothing they can do about it.

The Muslim New Year is called *Muharram,* which is the name of the first month of the Muslim moon-time calendar, but Muharram is not a big party time for Muslims. Some Muslims remember this as the time when Husayn ben Ali, the grandson of Muhammad, was killed, and so they do not eat anything on the tenth day of the first month. This fasting holiday is called *Ashurah.*

Because of the "times they are a-changin' " message of the holidays, religions help us to see the change of the seasons in nature as a time to give thanks for all that nature gives us and a time to remember that no matter how dark and cold it is outside, the sun is gonna shine again. This is a good message that gives us hope and humility when we need it most.

The second message of the holidays has nothing to do with the seasons. It has to do with holy history. Holy history is the way people in a religion remember what happened long ago. Let's say the guy who was the main teacher in a religion, the main prophet, was born on a certain day or died and went to heaven on a certain day; those days would become special days in that religion.

Some of the holidays in religions celebrate things that we *know* happened, and some of the holidays celebrate things that we *believe* happened. Here's an example of this. There are stories about Moses and Jesus and Muhammad that are part of the holy history of Judaism, Christianity, and Islam. We can't say that we *know* that these things really happened because there really is no proof for them other than the stories in the holy books. Stories about miracles are like this. The only proof that Moses split the Red Sea, that Jesus rose from the dead, or that Muhammad went to heaven on his horse are the stories from the Hebrew Bible, the New Testament, or the Quran. This does not mean that these things did not happen. It only means that we can't *know* they happened, because we have only the proof from the books. We can *believe* that these things happened because we *trust* that the holy books are true, but believing is not the same as knowing. Anyway, religions teach us about holy history, which has some stuff in it we can know and some stuff in it we can believe. Both knowing and believing help us to grow wise in the world.

The Birthday of the Big Teacher

One of the most common religious holidays is the birthday of the big teacher. The biggest birthday party in the world is Christmas. It is a beautiful story, and when you add in decorating the Christmas tree, getting together with family, going to church, singing Christmas carols, and giving presents . . . well, it is a really great holiday! There is just one problem with Christmas and with some other big holidays: *Sometimes the party for the holiday gets bigger than the lesson of the holiday.* You know, Christmas is not about being given presents. Christmas is about being given Jesus. When you forget that, you forget the main meaning of Christmas.

In Islam there is a holiday that celebrates the birth of the big teacher of Islam, Muhammad. Muhammad's birthday is called *al-Mawlid annabawi ash'shareef.* The Mawlid is on the twelfth day of the Muslim month of Rabi. The month of Rabi also has holidays when Muslims remember the day Muhammad went up to heaven on his horse, as well as the day he died. The custom of this month is for adults to study the Quran a lot, which is a very good way to honor the prophet Muhammad, who taught so much to so many people. Muslim children celebrate the birthday of the prophet by putting on skits and plays in school that show scenes from the prophet's life.

Buddhists celebrate the birth of the Buddha in a springtime holiday called *Wesak,* which we said a little about already. Wesak comes every year on the fourteenth to the sixteenth day of the sixth month in the Buddhist calendar. Usually that falls during May, but since Buddhists use moon-time calendars and not sun-time calendars, Wesak changes from year to year. Wesak is like Buddha Day. It is the holiday that celebrates the birth, enlightenment, and death of Siddhartha Gautama. Wesak also celebrates the way the Buddha just kind of disappeared after teaching everything he had to teach. He didn't really die; he just went to the pure world of nirvana, which is the place where all Buddhas go when they have finished what they were supposed to do on planet earth.

In Thailand, Wesak is a big national holiday. The king and queen march in a parade around the temple of the Emerald Buddha. The parade is at night when there is a full moon. Everybody carries candles, and the temple is decorated with candles and flowers.

One of the things that makes the festivals celebrating the birth of the big teachers so happy is that most of the guys never died. Moses got taken up from Mount Nebo right straight to God without dying. Buddha went to nirvana alive from the Bo tree. Jesus is one big teacher who died, but he came back to life after three days. Muhammad definitely died and did not come back to life, but while he was alive, he went up to heaven on his horse, al-Barak.

Judaism and Hinduism do not have a day for celebrating the birth of the prophet. This is probably because Judaism and Hinduism do not have *one* big teacher, as Buddhism, Christianity, and Islam do.

The Fasting Time

Almost all religions tell us to stop eating for a while during the year. Fasting really means not eating or drinking anything, but that can get to be impossible, especially since some fasts last a month! Usually a fast means not eating *some* things or not eating anything during certain times of the day.

Fasting is very common in religions because it helps you to purify your body. Fasting gives you a chance to get rid of some of the junk you have let into your stomach, and this helps you to think about getting rid of some of the junk you have let into your life. Fasting gives you a chance to concentrate on praying without worrying about who is going to fix lunch. Fasting is also a way for you to remember how good it is to be able to eat and to thank God for food and eating and living.

Jews fast on several days. The most well known Jewish fast day is *Yom Kippur,* which is ten days after the New Year's holiday, Rosh Hashana. Jews are supposed to spend ten days making up with people they have hurt during the past year and trying to get it together to be a better person during the next year. The fast of Yom Kippur is spent in synagogue, praying all day and asking God to forgive us for our sins. The fast is only for Jews over thirteen, and it is a fast that starts the night before the day of Yom Kippur and lasts until sundown on Yom Kippur. No water or food of any kind is eaten during this fast. This is not the only fast day in the Jewish calendar, but it is by far the most important.

The Muslims fast for the month of Ramadan, which is the ninth month of the Muslim moon-time calendar. At first the Muslims fasted on Ashurah, which, like Yom Kippur, is on the tenth day of the New Year. The Shiite Muslims still do that. But the big fast time became Ramadan. The fast lasts for the twenty-nine days of the month. No food or drink of any kind is taken during the daytime. Then at night, after prayers, a big dinner is eaten, and in the morning, a very big, very early breakfast, to get in some food before the sun comes up.

The fast of Ramadan is for all Muslims who are adults, who are not traveling, and who are healthy. This is a big thing. Islam and Judaism and most all religions teach that fasting is not as important as staying healthy, so if you are sick, you must take care of yourself and wait until you are better again to fast.

Ramadan ends with a big party that can last for up to four days. The holiday is called *id-al fitr* or *al-id al-saghir*. In addition to big meals, this holiday is celebrated by giving money to the poor and taking food to friends. People who can afford to also get new clothes to wear at this time. The Indonesian Muslims have a neat custom for this holiday. Children go to their parents and grandparents and kneel down in front of them and ask them for a blessing and say they are sorry for the bad things they have done (like cursing or not picking up their socks).

Buddhism is into fasting more than most religions. All Buddhist monks fast every day, not eating or drinking anything from noon until the next morning. Buddhist monks eat only one meal a day. Really, this Buddhist fasting makes a lot of sense. Most of us eat too often and too much, and when we eat, we stuff ourselves like pigs. It's a good thing to cut back on food and do more reading and singing.

The Christian fast time is *Lent*. It is the forty days before Easter. Lent celebrates the forty days that Jesus spent alone and fasting in the desert before he came back to be with people again. Lent is fast time for different Christians in different ways. Most Christians fast on Ash Wednesday (the first day of Lent) and on

Good Friday (the day Jesus died). Some Christians fast every Friday during Lent and some Christians eat no meat or cheese during Lent.

The Big-Time Day

Most every religion has a holiday that celebrates a time when something happened long ago that was so important it has to be remembered every year at the time it happened. That is a big-time day.

The Jewish big-time day is *Passover,* which comes during the moon month of Nisan. Passover is the holiday that celebrates the time the Jews got out of Egypt. This is called the Exodus from Egypt, and it is the time that Jews believe they turned into a free people, no longer slaves.

Passover is celebrated with a meal called the *seder* that has special foods and special prayers and special songs and is kind of like a play in which everybody helps to act out the story of the Exodus. People at the meal eat horseradish to remember the bitterness of slavery, they eat things dipped in salt water to remember the tears of slavery, and they eat parsley to remember the new green things of spring. They even eat a mixture of apples and wine and cinnamon and nuts to remember the stuff that stuck the bricks together in the buildings they had to build for Pharaoh. The seder also has happy foods in it. There are four cups of wine people drink during the meal to remember how good it felt to be free.

One of the nicest parts of the seder is how it begins. Everybody says, "Let all who are hungry come and eat." Holiday meals are great, but if we don't remember those people who have nothing to eat, then our eating is selfish. Holidays help us to give up being selfish and to share our blessings.

Matzoh is the special bread baked for Passover. Matzoh is made of just flour and water and nothing else. Matzoh has to be baked within eighteen minutes after the water and flour are mixed together. The matzoh comes out flat and looking (and tasting) kind of like a page from the telephone book. Jews eat no other kind of bread for the whole week of the Passover holiday to remind themselves of how their ancestors had to run to get out of Egypt, how they did not have time even to let the bread rise.

The Muslim big-time day is *id ul-Adhah*, or as most Muslims call it, *al-id al-kabir*, "the great festival." This holiday is celebrated on the tenth day of the moon month of Hijja, and it is part of the pilgrimage holiday. Even Muslims who are not going to Mecca celebrate this great holiday, which lasts for about four days. Muslims try to dress up in something new for the great festival. This holiday celebrates the Bible story that tells of Abraham's test, when God asked him to sacrifice his son. When Muslims tell the story, they say it was Abraham and Ishmael who went up the mountain. (In the Hebrew Bible, it is Abraham and Isaac who went up the mountain.)

Muslims believe that Ishmael was their ancestor. To remember this story, Muslims eat a roasted sheep split up into three parts. One part is for the family, one part is for relatives, and one part is for the poor. It is always nice to have something in a holiday to help the poor, because holiday times are really sad for poor people, especially children, who otherwise don't ever get a chance to eat the holiday foods and get the holiday presents.

God did not give us holidays so that we could stuff our faces and buy things for ourselves. God gave us holidays to hold on to time and to thank God for every good thing we take for granted day by day. Sharing what we have is a *big* part of what makes holidays great. If you don't share, you have missed one of the main points of the holidays.

The Christian big-time day is *Easter.* The meaning of Easter is really the meaning of Christianity. Easter is all about what the Resurrection of Jesus meant to the world. It meant that the sin of Adam (disobeying God) was wiped away from the world and that the Kingdom of God was open to all people. Easter is a real big-time day for Christians.

Easter is a moon-time holiday, like Passover. Easter is always on the Sunday following the new moon after the vernal equinox. (The best way to figure this out is to open up a calendar and look around in April or March and see when Easter is. The other good way to know when Easter is coming is to call up a priest or a minister or a person who makes chocolate bunnies. They know for sure.)

Like the Jewish holiday of Passover, Easter is celebrated with a special meal, called the *Eucharist.* The Eucharist meal is made up of bread that looks like matzoh (some Christians use bread for the Eucharist that is more like real bread) and wine. The bread of the Eucharist meal helps Christians receive the body of Jesus, who died to get rid of their sins. The wine of the Eucharist is to receive the blood of Jesus.

Many Christians believe that when a priest says a blessing over the bread and the wine that the bread and wine really change into the body and the blood of Jesus. Only a priest can do this, and it is one of the most special and holy things that happens for a Christian. Almost all Christians eat the bread and drink the wine of the Eucharist on Easter, and some Christians—Roman Catholics and Eastern Orthodox and many Anglican and Lutheran Christians—take the Eucharist every Sunday or even more, to remember the really big thing that happened on Easter.

Easter is really more of a week than a day. The holy week of Easter starts with Palm Sunday, which is the day Jesus came to Jerusalem. Holy Thursday was the day Jesus went to the seder meal that was his last supper. It is also the day Christians believe Jesus started the priesthood and the Eucharist. Then comes Good Friday, which is the day Christians believe that Jesus died by being nailed up on a cross by the Roman army, who were ordered to do so by Pontius Pilate. Holy Saturday is the day the church receives people who want to be Christians, and there is a Eucharist meal, which is called a *Mass,* on Saturday night. Easter Sunday is the day Christians believe that Jesus came alive and rose up from the dead. There is also a holiday forty days after Easter called Ascension, which celebrates when Jesus went back to heaven after spending forty days showing his followers that he was alive again and telling them what to do until he came back from heaven.

This idea that you have to get ready for a big holiday is part of most religions. Judaism has ten days to get ready for the big holiday of Yom Kippur. Muslims have ten days to get ready for the fast of Ashurah and a whole month of fasting in Ramadan to get ready for the holiday that ends the fast. Buddhists have about three weeks to get ready for Wesak. And Christians have about a month in the period called Advent to get ready for Christmas and six weeks of Lent to get ready for Easter.

All religions know that it is real hard to just go from a regular day right into the day of a big holiday. You need to get ready, you need to prepare. You need to think about what is coming so that when it comes, you will be there with all your heart and with all your mind and with all your soul.

CHAPTER 10

What Are the Holy Times in My Life?

When you really think about it, life is different for each of us. Of course, we all have different faces and fingerprints, and many of us have different names. Most important of all, we have different DNA, which means that when you look inside the cells in our bodies, the stuff you find sloshing around in there is different from that of every other person who was ever born and who will ever be born. Just like snowflakes, each and every one of us is special and different.

On the other hand, think about how many ways we are all alike. All of us get born (or else we wouldn't be here), and all of us die (or else nobody could ever use our room). And when you think about it, there are lots of other things that happen to just about everybody: dropping something heavy on your toe, getting a cold, losing some of your stuff, finding somebody else's stuff, eating something so good you can hardly believe it, getting hugged, getting kissed, falling in love. These are just some of the things that, like getting born and dying, happen to pretty much everybody at some time or another.

One of the things religions do is to help us remember and say thank you to God for the times in our lives that we all go through. Religions do not have anything special for us when we get a cold, but when it comes to being born and dying and other important times like that, religion is a big help.

The things we do for the special times of our lives are called *rituals,* and every religion has them. Here are some of the special times of life and the rituals that go along with them.

Birth

Being born is the first time in life that all religions make extra special. The special birth rituals remind adults that when we were born, there were people who loved us so much that they brought us into their family. Bringing the baby into the religion is the second thing that religions do.

Many religions also do things to keep the baby safe for a few days until it's given a name. Holding off for a few days before giving a name is one way religions have of waiting to see if the baby will be all right. You don't want to name the baby and have a big party and get everybody excited if the kid is not going to make it, so all religions wait.

This waiting time is filled with all sorts of rituals. Religions have ways of helping us deal with what we don't understand, and one of the things we don't understand is why some babies turn out healthy and others get sick and die. Some of the old protect-the-baby rituals have lasted a long time. Jews tie a red ribbon on the baby's crib. Chinese Buddhists hang a piece of raw ginger from the door and tie a charm from a Buddhist temple around the kid's neck at birth, while the mother burns incense to keep the baby safe. In Japan, a mother who is about four months away from giving birth goes to a Shinto temple and does the *Iwata-obi* ceremony to protect her baby from evil spirits. Shintoism teaches that the soul of a baby goes into the body of the baby at this time. In this ceremony the mother has a piece of silk cloth wound around her. In Hinduism, the baby is held by the father as he whispers a *mantra* in the baby's ear, which is a kind of sacred word that is supposed to protect the baby.

Another reason to wait before giving a name is to teach that there is a big difference between being born and coming into the religion. Birth automatically brings you into a family, but you still need to be brought into the religion. Sometimes people come into a religion when they are adults, but usually they come as babies. The point is that being born and coming into the religion are not the same. Being born gives you a life, but it does not give you a way to live your life.

There are different ways that religions show that you have come into the religion. Sometimes our names are a sign of our religion. Someone named CHRISTopher or CHRISTine is almost sure to be a Christian (you can guess why). Someone named Abdul is usually a Muslim, because the name Abdul means "a person who loves Muhammad." Names are one way we give a sign to other people about where we came from.

Many babies are named after somebody in the family. Lots of times it is somebody who has died. This is a nice thing to do because it helps the memory of the dead person live on. Sometimes the baby is named after somebody living. This is nice because that person can look out for the baby.

The naming ceremonies are very different from one religion to another. In China, on the third day after birth, mothers take their child to be washed by the Buddhist priests. Then they dress the baby in nice clothes and wave an open lock over the baby from head to foot. When the lock reaches the ground, it is closed. This is to show that the baby is locked to the earth. Then white paper money is burned and sweet rice balls and cakes are offered. On the twenty-ninth or thirtieth day of a kid's life, the baby's grandma takes the kid to the hall of a Buddhist temple. There the family's ancestors are remembered, and a party is held in honor of the baby naming.

Buddhists in southeast Asia call in an astrologer for the naming ceremony. Astrologers are the people who think that the way that the stars and the planets move changes our lives. Hindus rub the baby's tongue with a mixture of *ghee*, which is a kind of butter, and honey. This idea of touching a baby's lips or tongue with something sweet is also in other religions. In Judaism the baby is given some sweet red wine at the naming ceremony. The sweet wine is to ask God that the baby be given a sweet life.

After a baby is born in Japan, there are four ceremonies, one each on the night of the baby's birth and the nights of the third, fifth, and seventh days. On the eighth day there is a party, and the baby gets a name from a godparent. Lots of religions have godparents, who are supposed to take care of the child if anything happens to the parents and who are supposed to make sure that the child is taught about the religion even if the parents get lazy about it.

In Christianity the naming ceremony is called a *baptism*. Baptism is the ceremony to bring a person, usually a baby, into Christianity. It's interesting that the Christians who are called Baptists do not believe in baptizing babies. They believe it is better to wait until the ceremony means something to the person, so they only baptize adults.

In a baptism the person is dunked in water or water is sprinkled or poured over his or her head. Christians believe that the water is a sign of how Jesus came to wash away sin. The father

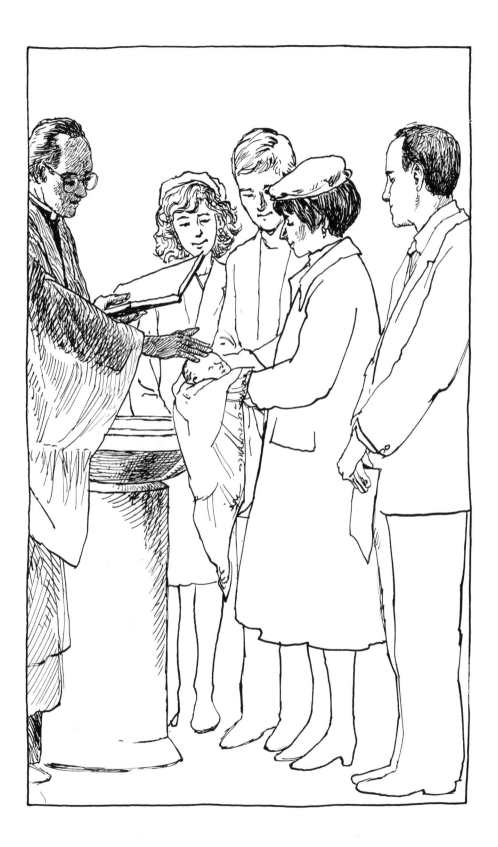

and mother go to church with the godparents, a godfather and a godmother, and friends and relatives. The priest or minister prays, reads from the Bible, and asks the parents, "What name do you wish to give to your child?" Christian parents usually choose a first and middle name at baptism.

There is a prayer of the faithful and a prayer of exorcism. Exorcism is to keep evil spirits away. The priest or minister then pours a little oil over the forehead of the baby. Sometimes grandparents and great-grandparents will join in this pouring of the oil, which is called *anointing*. This ritual goes back to the time just after Jesus, when Christians baptized using oil. Parents then promise to raise their child as a good Christian. The priest or minister will then baptize the child by pouring water over the child's forehead and saying, "I baptize you in the name of the Father and of the Son, and of the Holy Spirit."

The godparents promise to raise the child as a Christian if the parents die. In some churches the godfather then receives a candle called a *baptismal candle*, which has a triangle painted on it. The triangle stands for the Father, Son, and Holy Spirit. The candle has the first and the last letters of the Greek alphabet painted on it, *alpha* and *omega*. This is the sign that for Christians, Jesus is the beginning and the end of all life. The candle also has a dove on it. That bird is the sign of the Holy Spirit flying down from heaven to go into the child. The godfather lights the baptismal candle and gives it to the parents. Then the godmother receives a baptismal garment, which she places over the child's head. This garment is white and has the sign of Jesus and the flowing waters of baptism on it.

The menus for naming parties in all the religions are neat. Usually there is some kind of fish served, because fish is a symbol of life, and there are lots of fish. In Japan the naming party has rice cooked with red beans, a cooked fish called sea bream, and sake, Japanese rice wine. In Jewish naming parties there is lox, other smoked fish, and bagels and cream cheese. In China the naming party has fish and rice but also eggs, which are dyed a red color and are sent by friends and relatives for the party, along with other food and gifts.

When a baby boy is born there is some skin that covers the top of his penis. Jews and Muslims have this skin cut off. So do some African tribes and Polynesian people. The ancient Mayas and Aztecs in Peru and Mexico also did this, and some American Indians did and continue to do this. The name of this practice is *circumcision.* Muslims used to circumcise their sons when they were about seven years old, but many people have it done earlier these days, because circumcision is not a real great birthday present for a seven-year-old. Muslim boys are taken to the place where they are circumcised wearing a veil. For Christians, being circumcised is not something Christianity teaches they have to do, but most of them do it anyway for health reasons.

For Jews, there is a big religious circumcision ceremony called the *brit milah.* In the 17th chapter of the Book of Genesis, God tells Abraham to circumcise himself and his son Isaac, and to have all boy babies of the Jewish people circumcised on the eighth day after birth. For Jews, circumcision is the sign of the covenant between God and the Jewish people forever—which means that it is a sign of connection between every new Jewish baby boy born now and Abraham, who was born way back then.

The person who does the circumcision is called a *mohel* (pronounced *moil*). The mohel comes to the baby boy's house in the morning of the eighth day unless the baby is sick, in which case the circumcision is put off until the baby is well. The baby is brought to the mohel on a pillow by the godfather, and then the father says a prayer to thank God for the commandment to circumcise his son. The baby does not say thank you! After the circumcision, the baby is given a Hebrew name and returned to the mother, who is usually in another room biting her fingernails.

Becoming a Grown-up

Many religions have rituals to divide the time when we are kids from the time when we are grown-ups. These rituals show that the child has grown up enough to be a part of the adult community. In places where people work early in life, they may get married right after they go through the becoming-a-grown-up rituals. In other places they still live like children for years after these rituals. Knowing when you are born or when you die is easy, but knowing when you are a grown-up is the hardest change of life to pin down.

Jews have a very important becoming-a-grown-up ritual for boys, called *bar mitzvah*. It happens on the boy's thirteenth birthday. On that day he celebrates being a Jewish man by reading from the Torah scroll. Reading from the Torah scroll is the hardest and most important grown-up ritual in Judaism, and no Jewish person under thirteen is allowed to do it. By preparing to read from the Torah scroll on his thirteenth birthday, the Jewish boy is saying to all the other grown-ups in the Jewish community, and, most importantly, to God, "I am *really* ready to be a good Jewish grown-up." Even if a boy of thirteen does not read from the Torah, he is still a bar mitzvah and still a Jewish adult from that day on. The first *bat mitzvah* (a becoming-a-grown-up ritual for girls that is equivalent to a bar mitzvah) took place nearly seventy-five years ago, and since then lots of Jewish girls in synagogues that are not Orthodox have read from the Torah just like boys. Orthodox Jews still only let men read from the Torah.

After the reading from the Torah the family usually has a party for the bar or bat mitzvah child who has just become a grown-up. Sometimes the parties are small and nice, sometimes the parties are big and nice, and sometimes the parties are big and silly. Most of the parties have chopped liver, but now lots of them also have sushi. Keeping parties smaller than the rituals they are supposed to celebrate is one of the hardest things for all religions in our time.

Christians have a becoming-a-grown-up ritual called *confirmation*. Confirmation is kind of like a second baptism for Christian kids. They go to special classes and they study about the teachings of Jesus and their church, and then they have a special confirmation ceremony that says they are ready to become good grown-up Christians. There is no set time for the confirmation ritual in Christianity. Orthodox Christians do it right at the time of baptism. Protestant and Roman Catholic Christians do it when the child is a teenager. Most Roman Catholics celebrate confirmation at about thirteen. It's not the age but the getting ready that is important to Christians.

Confucianism in China has a neat ceremony for becoming an adult. After checking the star charts to find out what year and day you become a man, you go to the top steps of the eastern side of the Confucian temple and stand there in front of your family and guests while three hats are placed on your head, one at a time. Each hat stands for a part of your life, and each hat is more beautiful than the last hat. After all three hats are put on in the *capping ceremony* the new man goes to greet his mother and brothers and cousins and the rest of his family as a grown-up.

For the Brahman Hindu boys there is a becoming-a-grown-up ceremony called the *upanayana,* which means "new birth." The upanayana happens when the Brahman Hindu boy is eight years old. Other Hindus have their becoming-a-grown-up rituals at eleven or twelve. The Brahman Hindu gets a holy thread that is worn over the left shoulder and under the right arm. Girls used to have a becoming-a-grown-up celebration, but not anymore. For many girls, getting married is their way of becoming a grown-up in this religion.

Lots of religions think of becoming a grown-up as a new birth. The grown-up Hindu Brahman is called a *dvija*, which means "born twice." When a child is born, the birth rituals are done *to* him or her, but in the becoming-a-grown-up rituals the things are done *by* him or her. That is what growing up is all about. It is about learning to do grown-up things for yourself. Every religion needs its kids to say, "Don't worry! We care as much about our religion as you adults did, and we will keep it safe and keep it going when you are gone." The becoming-a-grown-up rituals give kids a chance to say that, and they give adults a chance to hear that—and then everybody goes out and has a party. What a great idea!

Marriage

On the Buddhist wedding day in China or in Japan, the bride is taken in a big parade to the house of the groom, which is where the wedding happens. The bride and groom kneel down and pray in front of the house altar of the groom's ancestors. Then the bride and groom hold two fancy cups tied together with red thread and drink a drink made of wine and honey. Then they go to a big party where the bride and groom run around serving other people. Later the groom goes to his bride's family's house and prays before her house altar.

In Islam, the closest male relative to the bride, called a *wali*, takes the gifts given to the bride, called *mahr*, and writes a marriage contract, which is the thing that makes her the wife of the

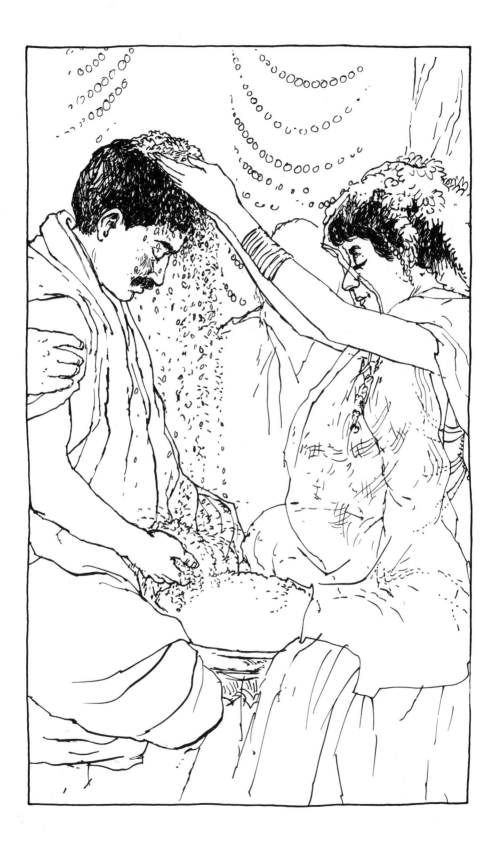

groom. The man must give the woman something made of gold. The woman gives the man clothing or some other gift. The wedding ceremony is usually at a *masjid*, the Muslim house of prayer.

The party after an Islamic wedding is called the *walima*. The walima has lots of good grilled meat and sweets and also has loud music. The day after the wedding, the groom is supposed to give another party.

The wedding ceremony in Judaism usually happens in a synagogue, but it doesn't have to. The bride and groom stand under a canopy called a *hupah*, which stands for the way God shelters us and also for the home they will make together. The groom puts a ring on the bride's finger. The ring is pure gold with no diamonds in it and with no holes in it, except the hole your finger goes through. Then the groom says, *"hare at mekudeshet li b'tabat zo k'dat moshe v'yisrael,"* which means, more or less, "With this ring you are made holy and special to me as my wife, and this is just the way Moses and the people of Israel have always done things." In some Jewish weddings the bride puts a ring on the groom and says the same kind of thing. They drink twice from a wine cup or from two wine cups, and the rabbi says prayers. Then the groom smashes a glass under his foot and kisses the bride. Everybody shouts *"mazal tov!"* which means "good luck." Then people go to the wedding party.

In Christianity, the wedding usually happens in a church. The groom and his people come in first. The groom is at the front of the church, and everybody else is at the back of the church, blocking his escape. The bride comes in holding on to the arm of her father, who gives her to the groom. The bride and groom kneel in some churches, they stay standing in others, and in some churches the bride and groom sit down. The priest or minister reads some prayers and gives a brief talk in which he or she tries out some new material and then the groom says to the bride: "I, (the groom says his name), take you, (the groom says the name of the bride), to be my wife. I promise to be true to you in good times and in bad, in sickness and in health. I will love you and honor you all the days of my life." Then the bride says the same thing. Then the groom places the wedding ring on the left-hand ring finger of the bride. He says, "Take this ring as a sign of my love and fidelity. In the name of the Father and of the Son and of the Holy Spirit. Amen." The bride does the same thing. Then they are hitched.

Wedding parties take place in every religion. They are important because they tell the community that a marriage has happened. They are also important because they give families and relatives from the groom's side and from the bride's side a chance to get to know each other, if they haven't already. At weddings people learn that it is not good to be alone, that babies are a good thing, and that love leads us to marriage if it is real love.

Death

Funerals are the religious ways of saying good-bye to someone whose life on earth has ended. When you think about it, funerals are one of the things that make us different from animals. One of the things that all religions teach is that death is not the end of us. Death is just the end of our bodies, not the end of our souls.

There are lots of different kinds of funerals, but they all do the same type of thing. Funerals give the family and friends of the dead person a chance to get together and cry and laugh and remember the dead person. Funerals give people a chance to learn what a religion has to say about death. Funerals also give the family a place, maybe a grave or a river or some other place, where they can come and remember the dead person. And funerals give everybody a chance to think about just how important it is to be thankful for being alive.

Death is the same for all of us. It's only the funerals that are different. Lots of religions bury dead people in the ground in places called cemeteries. Jews do this, and so do Christians and Muslims. Some people do this because the Hebrew Bible said that Adam, the first person, was made by God from some red earth. So because Adam was made from earth, it seems right to return people to the earth after they die. Some folks think this is spooky or even a little scary, but we think it is just right. Burial shows that we are all a part of the earth. We come from it, and we go back to it. "Dust you are and to dust you shall return." (Genesis 3:19) That's the way Jews and Christians and Muslims see it.

Jews bury their dead right away. They are supposed to bury a dead person the very next day after the person dies. Sometimes Jews wait a little longer than that because some relatives have to fly in for the funeral, but fast burials are still a Jewish thing. Muslims also bury the dead right away, and they bury the dead facing Mecca. After the burial, Muslims give food to the poor.

Christians wait a while to bury the dead person. Some Christians have something called a *wake*, which usually lasts from one to three days. A wake is a time for the dead person's family to sit around the coffin and say prayers and think about the good things the person did when he or she was alive. The funeral happens after the wake. For some Christians the funeral is always in a church, but for others it doesn't have to be in a church. Christians often bury the dead, but they also sometimes burn up the body of the dead person until only ashes are left; this is called *cremation*. Jews and Muslims do not cremate the dead. At the burial, Jews shovel earth into the grave, but Christians usually do not shovel earth. Christians can bury more than one person in the same grave site, but Jews do not do this.

Some Hindus bury their dead. Children, holy men, and poor people are buried, but most Hindus cremate their dead and throw the ashes into a holy river. Many Hindus travel to the city of Banaras when they are about to die. Hindus believe that if they die in Banaras and have their ashes thrown into the Ganges they will get *moksha*, which is getting free of the world and not having to be reborn ever again. The close friends of the dead person carry the body to the cremation place by the river, and the oldest son marches in front.

Hindu cremation happens by putting the body of the dead person, which is wrapped up in cloth, on top of wood with wood branches over it. Then fires are lit around the body. One fire is to the northwest. Another fire is to the southwest, and the third fire is to the southeast. They watch to see which fire reaches the body first, because this is a sign of what kind of karma the person had. The people who take care of the cremations are called *candalas*. After the family returns from the cremation, they will not eat or drink very much for ten days to a month.

Buddhists also cremate their dead. Some Buddhists believe the Buddha was cremated by the Malla tribe of Kusinagara when he died. Ananda, the Buddha's student, told them to wrap the body in five hundred layers of new cloth and soak him in oil and then cremate the body. The bones of the Buddha went into shrines. Today Buddhists in Sri Lanka mostly bury the dead, but in southeast Asia most Buddhists cremate the dead. Buddhists are very quiet at funerals. They say prayers for forty-nine days.

CHAPTER II

Why Do Religions Split Up?

—

Religions split up because somebody in the religion says, "I know best what this religion really teaches." Then another person says, "Are you nuts? You don't know anything. I know it best!" Different people in the same religion each think that they know best what the religion really teaches. If the split is real deep, then a brand-new religion may get started. That happened when Christianity broke away from Judaism. That break happened because people could not agree about whether Jesus was the Messiah.

Sometimes there is a smaller split in a religion. The religion holds together, but just barely. That is when you get *denominations* in a religion instead of a whole new religion. Big religions almost always split up into denominations, but so do some small religions. Let's look at the parts of each religion and try to learn why they are parts of the same religion and not new religions.

The Parts of Judaism

There are four types of Judaism, and they are called *movements*, not denominations: Orthodox Judaism, Reform Judaism, Conservative Judaism, and Reconstructionist Judaism.

Orthodox Judaism was the only kind of Judaism until about 200 years ago. That is when Judaism started to split apart. It split up because that was when Jews had a choice about what kind of Jews they wanted to be. Before 200 years ago, the Orthodox rabbis had control over the way Jews practiced their religion. They had this power because the kings and queens and tsars of Europe gave it to them, but when religion began to be taken out of governments, Jews and Christians had more freedom to be just the kind of Jews and Christians they wanted to be.

Today only about ten percent of Jews are Orthodox. Being an Orthodox Jew means that you have to follow strict rules for the Sabbath Day. This means you can't go anywhere in your car. You can't turn on a light in your house, and you can't answer the telephone. If you are really Orthodox, you can't eat out in most restaurants, because you have to eat only kosher food, and most restaurants don't serve kosher food.

Orthodox Judaism sounds very strict with lots of rules, but it is also very beautiful. Staying home with your family for one day a week is a good idea. Not working on the Sabbath is a really good idea; it makes the day very peaceful and the family much closer. Not running around buying things is a good idea. Praying and studying are good ideas. The Sabbath is very real for Orthodox Jews, and that is very beautiful. Also, the special rules keep Orthodox Jews from ever forgetting that they are Jewish, and it gives them a way of sticking together. The most beautiful thing about Orthodox Judaism is the way it makes all the parts of life holy for God. But this is still a lot to ask of people who want to be a part of the modern world, and that is why it is the smallest part of Judaism.

There are some Orthodox Jews who are called *Hasidim.* The Hasidim are the Jews with the black coats, black hats, and beards. The Hasidim are different from other Orthodox Jews because they never send their children to public schools or college. They only go to school with other Hasidim, so they are even more separated from the outside world than the other Orthodox Jews, who are pretty separated themselves.

The other movements in Judaism (Reform, Conservative, and Reconstructionist) have differences, but these are really not that important. The main difference in Judaism is between Orthodox and all the other movements. Followers of all the other movements in Judaism do these things: Women become rabbis and *cantors* (the singers of Jewish prayers); men and women sit together in the prayer service; they eat in nonkosher restaurants; and they will probably answer the phone on the Sabbath.

These movements in Judaism treat men and women the same, and that is a good thing for most Jews. By making it easier to be Jewish, these movements in Judaism get more people in them, but they have the problem of making Judaism too easy. Whenever you change a strict religion so that people can live in the world without problems, there is a danger of changing the religion so much it loses all its important parts, and people forget that God wants a lot from them. But if you make a religion too hard, you drive people away. Most people like to have choices in their lives, and since the non-Orthodox movements give them more choices, they are the biggest parts of Judaism.

The Parts of Christianity

There are many kinds of Christians in the world: Roman Catholics, Anglicans, Protestants, and Orthodox Christians. All Christians, no matter what part of Christianity they belong to, believe this: Jesus was the Son of God and the Messiah who came to earth to die for our sins; he rose from the dead and went back to heaven but is going to come again some day.

That is what all Christians believe. But since Christianity is the biggest religion in the world (almost 1½ billion people!) and it has been around for almost two thousand years, you might figure that Christianity would split into a lot of parts, and you would be right.

Christianity became a big deal in the year 325, when the Roman Emperor Constantine converted himself and his whole empire to Christianity. This made Christianity the religion of a whole empire, and it made Christianity the biggest religion in the world just like that! To run the Church, Christians picked the bishop of Rome to be the boss. He was called the *pope*. The first pope was Peter, and up to the current pope, John Paul II, there have been 264 popes.

The first big split in Christianity came in the year 1054. In that year, some Christians who lived in Turkey wanted their leader, called a *patriarch*, to be equal to the pope. When the pope in Rome said "No way!" Christianity split into the Roman Catholic church and the Orthodox churches in the East, with the patriarch based in Constantinople (today called Istanbul).

One big difference between the two churches was that the Eastern churches did not listen to the pope in Rome, and the Roman church did not listen to the patriarch in Constantinople. In the East, priests can get married as long as they don't want to be bishops, but in the West they can't. In the East they use bread that really looks like bread for communion, and in the West they usually use bread that looks like flat round crackers. In the East they had prayers in the languages of the people, and in the West they used Latin for the prayers. But since 1963 even Roman Catholics have been praying in the languages of the people, so now this difference has gone away.

This East/West difference was the only split in Christianity until around the year 1517. That is the year when a monk named Martin Luther started complaining that the church in Rome was not honest anymore. He said that the popes had become rich and lazy and had lost touch with the people. He translated the Bible from Latin into German so that the ordinary person could read it. He put the prayers into the language of the people, and he said that nobody had to listen to the pope anymore. He said priests could get married, and he got married himself.

Martin Luther also said that only God, not priests or the pope, could forgive sins. He taught that believing in Jesus was the most important thing. He kept baptism and he kept communion, but he got rid of all the other things that Roman Catholics had to do. He added more singing to the service and more Bible readings.

The pope went crazy when he heard what Martin Luther was doing, and that is when Protestant Christianity split off from Roman Catholicism. Since the Protestant Reformation, which is what this split was called, there have been other Protestant denominations that have split off from the Lutherans, which is what the people who learned from Martin Luther were called. Calvinists, Presbyterians, Methodists, and Baptists also said that they were Protestants. King Henry VIII of England even started his own denomination when he could not get the pope to let him divorce his first wife, Catherine of Aragon, to marry Anne Boleyn. This Church of England that King Henry established spread and became a group of churches called the Anglican Communion. The part that came to America is called the Episcopal Church.

In the last 150 years there have been more and more kinds of Protestant Christianity splitting off from the Protestants who came before them. Today there are Congregationalists and Seventh-Day Adventists, Friends (also called Quakers), Evangelicals, and Pentecostals. Some of these Protestants wanted a simpler service than in Catholicism or Orthodox Christianity. Some did not want their ministers to have to report to a bishop, and some of the people wanted to be able to hire their ministers and to let their ministers get married. Some wanted to have women as ministers. Some, like the Quakers, did not want organ music, or any statues—including even the cross. Some wanted to sing more than in the old service of the Catholic church, and they wanted Christians to read the Bible more. For Protestants, the Bible was the rule book, not the teachings of the popes. The main thing is that Protestants wanted to have more to say about how their churches would be run.

The Parts of Buddhism

Buddhism began in India, but that is not the place where Buddhism lives now. Hinduism was just too big and too strong to let Buddhism grow in India. But in southeast Asia and in China and Japan and Tibet the teachings of the Buddha caught on. The spread of Buddhism out of India to the north and to the southeast is the reason why Buddhism has parts in it today. Northern Buddhism in China and Japan and Tibet is called *Mahayana* Buddhism. Southern Buddhism is called *Theravada* Buddhism. Theravada Buddhism believes that its teachings are closest to the teachings of the Buddha. They teach that everybody should try to be an *arhat*, which is somebody who has given up the things of this world by study of the *dharma*, the teachings of the Buddha, and by meditation.

Both kinds of Buddhism do not believe in God the way God is taught in the religions that go back to Abraham. But Mahayana Buddhism teaches that there is something bigger and better than us, which is even bigger and better than the Buddha. That something is called *tathata*, which means "suchness." Suchness is kind of like God. It is the truth and the law that rules the universe. Everything in the world is a part of tathata. In people, the tathata is kind of like our soul, but Mahayana Buddhists call it our Buddha nature.

The second big teaching in Mahayana Buddhism is the idea of the *bodhisattva.* The bodhisattva is a Buddha who came back from nirvana to earth to help people out. The bodhisattva is kind of like Jesus, but not exactly. He is a savior and a teacher of wisdom, and he has been to the high and holy place and has come back to tell us all what it is like and what we have to do to get there.

There is one more kind of Buddhism that is famous today, *Zen* Buddhism. This part of Buddhism started in China, where it is called *Ch'an*, but it really grew in Japan. The main teaching of Zen Buddhism is that you do not need any teaching. Meditation is a big part of all Buddhism, but it is a *very* big part of Zen. Meditation looks kind of like sleeping when you are awake, because like sleeping, meditation makes you comfortable and relaxed. But meditation is really very different than sleeping, because sleeping tunes you out and meditation tunes you in. Meditation helps you to understand what really matters and what is just noise. To meditate you may say a prayer word or phrase, called a *mantra*. Sometimes the mantra is said out loud, and sometimes it is said silently. In all mediation you breathe in a slow regular pattern, in and out, in and out, in and out, and then suddenly you understand everything. Now, if you breathe in and out and in and out like this and you *still* do not understand everything, keep breathing!

Zen Buddhism is a kind of *mysticism*. Mysticism is in all religions, and it teaches that you can get to know what is really real by just feeling it. You do not need to read it in a book or learn it in a classroom. You just have to be very quiet and let it come to you. Mysticism comes from people who want to get *really* close to God, or, for the mystics in the Eastern religions, people who want to get nirvana.

You know how some people paint just to pass the time. They like painting, but it is not the most important thing in their lives. Then there are painters who live only to paint. They think painting and eat painting and dream painting. Mystics are like the painters who really love painting, except they really love God, and God is all they really think about. They want to get close to God and know God and love God, and some of them want to disappear into God. Mystics are like the painters of the spirit.

The Parts of Islam

There are four parts of Islam, but all four parts believe the same big thing that all Muslims believe, which is called the *shahadah*. Remember that the shahadah says two things: There is no god but God (Allah); and Muhammad is the messenger of God. All Muslims of all the parts of Islam believe that the shahadah is true. All Muslims also believe that the Quran is from God, and they all have the same holidays, but beyond that there are some big differences in the parts of Islam.

Muslims are *Sunnis, Shiites, Kharijites,* or *Sufis.* The Kharijites are the smallest part of Islam. They live in Oman and southern Algeria. The Sunnis are the biggest part of Islam. More than eight out of every ten Muslims are Sunnis. The Sunni Muslims follow the *sunnah*, which are the teachings of Muhammad the way they see them. The full name of the Sunnis in Arabic is *ahl al-sunna wa'l-jama'ah*, which means "the people of the Sunna and the community." The Shiites teach that there is just one big imam for the world, and all Muslims should follow that imam. The Sunnis teach that there are many imams in the world.

The split between the Sunnis and the Shiites came right after the death of Muhammad, when the Muslims were fighting about who would be the *caliph*, which is the boss of Islam. A caliph is kind of like a pope. The Sunnis wanted the caliph to be Abu Bakir, who was a friend of Muhammad and from his tribe. The Shiites wanted Ali, who was the cousin and son-in-law of Muhammad, to be the first caliph. They wanted the caliph to come from the family of Muhammad, not just his tribe.

The Shiites got their name from *shi'at Ali*, which means "the followers of Ali." The Shiites also have parts. They divided up into the Twelve Imam Shiites, who are also called the *Imamis*, the *Ismailis*, and the *Zaydis*. The Muslims who took over in Iran after the Shah was kicked out in 1979 are Imamis. The Zaydis live only in Yemen. The Ismailis live in Egypt and Pakistan and India.

The Shiites also have an idea like the Christian and Jewish idea of the Messiah. This is the belief in the Twelfth Iman, who is alive and in the world but not yet in a human body (in Arabic this is called *gaybah*). This Twelfth Imam is going to get into a human body someday and tell everybody that he is the last imam and bring peace to the whole world. Another name for this last imam is the *Mahdi*.

Then there are Sufis. They are the Muslim mystics. The word

Sufi means "the guys who wear wool." They wear wool robes that have not been dyed and are real scratchy. Sufi Muslims own nothing, and they do not get married. The Sufis fast a lot, meditate a lot, and think deeply about Allah a lot. They believe what lots of mystics from all different religions believe: The best way to get close to God is to get away from the normal day-to-day life of the world.

The Parts of Hinduism

There are four parts of Hinduism: *Vaisnavites, Saivites, Saktis,* and *Smartas.* The Vaisnavites worship the god Vishnu. Most Hindus are either Vaisnavites or Saivites. The Vaisnavites believe in *bhakti,* which is giving yourself to Vishnu with all your heart and with all your soul. They also believe in *avataras,* which are the different shapes Vishnu takes when he comes into the world. The Vaisnavites are the ones who wrote the great Hindu book the Bhagavad-Gita.

The Vaisnavites are also the part of Hinduism that does not like the *caste* system, which teaches that some Hindus are lower than other Hindus just because of their birth. Instead of the caste markings on their foreheads, the Vaisnavites put two vertical white lines with a red line crossing them or two vertical white lines with a yellow dot in between. The Saivites mark their foreheads with three horizontal white lines.

The Saivites fast and meditate more than the Vaisnavites. Vishnu is the god of the Vaisnavites, and Shiva is the god of the Saivites. Vishnu is the god of the Hindus who creates things. Shiva is the destroyer god. The Saivites teach that the only way to keep Shiva from eating up the world is to fast and give up the pleasurable things of this world. Saivites definitely give up pleasure! Some of them cover their bodies with ashes. Some go

around with torn clothes and with long hair. Some lie on hot coals or sleep on nails. They also fast a lot.

The Saktis pray to a female god named Sakti, who they think made the world and gives power to the world, kind of like Mother Nature. They spend their time thinking about how the gods made the world.

The Smartas are named from the word that means "remember." They are the ones who taught Hinduism to poor people. They teach Hindus how to live and what to do.

CHAPTER 12

Who Works for God?

Working for God is great. The Boss is invisible. You get to go to a lot of great parties with good food, and you get to preach sermons where you tell other people how they should live and maybe throw in a few jokes. Then one day a family that is in your church or synagogue or masjid or temple or pagoda comes to you, and they ask, "Why did this person we love have to die?" And it is *you* who are supposed to explain why this happened. It is *you* who are supposed to make everything all better for them. This is when you understand that working for God can also be a very lousy job.

The people who work for God are *clergy*. Some clergy get paid for their work, and it's all they do. Some clergy do their clergy work for free and have other jobs to pay the rent. Nearly all the big religions have clergy who don't do anything else. They may have different titles, and they may do different things, but all the clergy persons are trying to do the same thing as well as they can: They are all trying to give us hope, and they are all trying to teach us about the religion so that we can do the right thing more than we do.

Lots of people have no idea how you get to be a clergy person, so in this chapter we are going to tell you just exactly how you go from being a kid to being a clergy guy or gal.

How Do You Become a Rabbi?

To become a rabbi, you have to be Jewish. You are Jewish if your mom was Jewish or if you convert to be a Jew. Some Jews today believe that if you only have a Jewish father that is enough to be Jewish if you are brought up Jewish, but somehow, someway you have to be Jewish to be a rabbi.

To be a rabbi you also need lots of Jewish education. You can get Jewish education two ways—go to a Jewish school, or go to any school and then go to a synagogue school after you get home from regular school or on the weekends.

Jewish schools start in first grade and go through high school. A school for Orthodox Jews is called a *yeshiva.* A school for Jews who are not Orthodox is called a Jewish day school. Only Jewish boys can go to a yeshiva. Orthodox Jewish girls can go to a Jewish school for girls but not a yeshiva, because Orthodox Jewish girls can't become rabbis. Jewish women from all the other parts of Judaism can become rabbis. They go with Jewish men to rabbi schools called *seminaries,* which is what all schools that teach clergy are called.

If you want to get into any of the seminaries, you have to go to high school and then you have to go to college and then, *after* college, you go to seminary for four or five or six years. Then you get a piece of paper that says: "This guy [or gal] is a *real* rabbi, and they can do all the rabbi things they want."

How Do You Become a Priest, Nun, or Brother?

If you want to be a priest, you first have to be one of three flavors of Christian: Roman Catholic, Episcopalian, or Orthodox. You get to be one of these flavors of Christian by getting baptized and confirmed. When you go to church and are old enough, you get religious instruction. If you really like what you are learning you might decide to become an altar server. In the Roman Catholic church, they used to have only altar boys, but as we were writing this book, that changed, and now girls can help the priest at the altar. The altar servers help the priest during the Mass. The server makes sure the priest has enough wine and water and bread.

Roman Catholic seminaries that train men to be priests who work in the local parishes, called *diocesan* priests, start after college and go for five years. For one of those five years you work in a parish with a diocesan priest to see if you like it.

If you don't want to be a diocesan priest and work in the parishes, you can be an *order* priest. An order is a group of priests or nuns or brothers (nuns and brothers are not priests, so they can't say Mass) who all try to live together and do God's work together and in the same way. Some orders, like the Franciscans, work with the poor; some, like the Jesuits and some Benedictines, teach; some, like the Maryknollers, are missionaries; and some, like the Trappists, pray a lot and in their spare time make great jelly and honey. All the orders in the Roman Catholic and Episcopal churches do holy work, and each order gives itself to God in its own special way. (If you want to get into the orders that live in the pretty mountains and make jelly and honey you might have to wait a while. If you want to join an order working with sick people in Calcutta, you can probably get in right away.)

If you are in an order, you give away all your stuff, and anything you earn goes to the order. If you are a diocesan priest, you get to keep what you make, but you are not going to make that much, so don't get too excited.

To become a brother or a nun you go to a religious school called a *novitiate*, where you study about the order. All nuns and brothers are part of an order, but as we said, not all priests are part of an order.

After seminary, you are ordained as a priest. You then need to get a parish of your own. If you are a Roman Catholic, the bishop, who is your boss, has to send you to a church. The people in the church don't have much say about who the bishop sends them. In the Episcopal church, the parish selects the priest, but the bishop has to approve the priest the parish selects.

Some religions let the people decide who will lead them and some don't. Both ways have something good and bad about them. People like to be able to pick their own religious leaders; however, when the clergy person is *not* picked by the people, he or she does not have to be worried about being fired by them. There is good and bad to each way, but the important thing is that if you look hard enough, you will find a place where you can find hope and learn about your religion in a way that is good for you.

One of the big things that everybody knows is that when a guy is ordained a priest in the Roman Catholic church, he cannot get married. This is a huge thing to give up, but there are good things about it along with the bad. The real good thing about priests not getting married is that they never have to take time away from their own families to help other people. This is one of the hard parts of being a married clergy person.

Episcopal priests can get married and Orthodox priests can

also get married, but Orthodox priests can get married only before they are ordained, and those who marry cannot become bishops.

How Do You Become a Minister?

If you want to be a minister, you first have to be a Protestant Christian. You get to be a Protestant by being baptized. Then you grow up and go to church and go to Sunday school to learn about what Christians believe.

There are so many kinds of Protestants that it is hard to say just one way that you get to be a minister. One of the ways you get to be a minister is like the way you get to be a priest or a rabbi. You go to high school and then college and then seminary. Many Protestant seminaries take three years after college, with one year spent working in a parish.

To get a job, if you are a minister, you go for an interview at a church, and the people of the church decide if they want to hire you. All ministers can get married and have a family.

In some Protestant churches, like the Pentecostal churches and some Southern Baptist churches, a person can become a minister as a kid! This is not usual, but it can happen if there is a kid who is really good at preaching and really wants to do the work of God.

Also, some Protestant ministers never went to any seminary, but they become ministers anyway. Going to a minister who has not gone to seminary is not for everybody. You would not go to somebody who called himself a doctor who never went to medical school. You would not go to a lawyer who never went to law school. Some folks ask, "How can you go to a minister who never went to seminary?" Well, the answer is that speaking the word of God is not like being a doctor or a lawyer. Sometimes

God speaks through simple people who have no education. Lots of the prophets in the Bible were simple folk. Amos was a tree cutter. So there can be something very wonderful about ministers who come to God *not* through the usual ways. Just be careful, because if ministers study at a seminary, the chances are that they know the teachings of Christianity, but if they just come from the neighborhood, what they teach might be their words but not the real true words of God. When you follow people to God, it is a good idea to look at what they do and how they live before you listen to what they say.

How Do You Become an Imam?

To be an imam you first have to be a Muslim. You get to be a Muslim by saying the shahadah, which most kids say when they are about seven years old. This ceremony is called *b'shmallah.*

You go to the masjid and learn the Quran and the prayers. If you like doing this, you keep on learning from older Muslims who know the Quran. These men are called *mullahs.* A mullah is a teacher of Islam. Men called *muftis* also teach the Quran, but muftis are mostly judges who decide about things for the religion for the leaders of Muslim countries. After you learn a lot, the Muslims in your masjid may come to you and ask you to lead prayers. This means that you are an imam for them. The person who knows the most about the Quran and who most lives the teachings of the Quran will be asked to be an imam.

You can see that being an imam is very different from being a priest or a minister or a rabbi. A Sunni imam never makes his living being an imam. He always has another kind of job. Also, being an imam is not a forever thing. You can be an imam and then let somebody else be an imam. Every masjid has an imam because every masjid has somebody to lead them in prayers.

For the Shiite Muslims, the imam is a much bigger deal. There is just one imam in the world at a time. This imam is kind of like the pope is for Roman Catholics. His followers believe that he is saying what Muhammad would say if he were here.

How Do You Become a Buddhist Monk?

To become a Buddhist monk you first have to become a Buddhist. To become a Buddhist you must say the Three Refuges, and they are: "To be safe I go to the Buddha. To be safe I go to the dharma. To be safe I go to the sangha." If you say this, you are a Buddhist. The Tibetan Buddhists add a Fourth Refuge: "To be safe I go to the Lama."

When you are about age four, your parents teach you how to fold your hands and legs in prayer. Buddhist families go to the Buddhist temple about once a week, but there is no special day they have to go, like the Sabbath for Jews and Christians. On the day they go to the temple, the parents do not eat anything. They also do not drink wine or listen to music or watch TV or wear makeup.

Buddhist monks own nothing and spend their day learning the teaching of the Buddha and begging for enough food to live. If you are ever in Laos or Thailand or any other Buddhist country, get up at dawn and see the villagers in the street waiting for the Buddhist monks to come take some rice for their rice bowls. Nobody speaks. The monks appear, get the rice, and then go back to the monastery in the mist of the early morning light.

Buddhist monks meditate a lot, sitting very quietly and breathing very slowly and making their minds clear. They have to be able to read the old Buddhist books in Sanskrit, which is the language in which they were written. Buddhist monks can perform wedding ceremonies and funerals, and of course they

teach people about Buddhism. Mainly monks try to live the kind of life that the Buddha lived. This is a lot like priests, brothers, and nuns, who try to live the kind of life that Jesus lived, and a lot like imams, who try to live the kind of life that Muhammad lived.

This is a very important thing to remember. Working for God means that you have to watch how you live, not just what you say. People who work for God have to be the kind of people that other folks can point to and say, "That is a holy person. That is a person who is trying to live just the way that God wants all of us to live, except he or she is really doing it." Buddhist monks have a neat way of doing this. Twice a month all the monks in the monastery come together and tell each other which rules they have broken. Then they ask to be forgiven, and they are forgiven.

In some parts of Buddhism the monks can be married and even live outside the monastery. This is the Mahayana way to be a monk. In the Theravada way of being a monk, you can't be married, and you have to live in the monastery. In all parts of Buddhism, women can become nuns. Mostly, any Buddhist who wants to be a monk for life does not get married. But *every* Buddhist man must live as a monk for at least one week and usually for a year sometime between age seven and age twenty. If the man is married, he needs to get the permission of his wife and kids to live as a monk for more than a few weeks. The *sangha* is the name of the group of monks who live together.

How Do You Become a Hindu Priest?

To be a Hindu priest, you have to be a Hindu. Some Hindus believe that you can convert to be a Hindu, but most Hindus say you have to be born a Hindu to be one. It is a complicated story we will tell you more about later.

The only Hindus who can become priests are Hindus of the Brahman caste, but not all Brahmans are priests. This caste is passed down from father to son, so you are a Brahman only if your dad was a Brahman. The son of a Brahman goes to school to learn the Sanskrit language, which is the holy language of the Hindus. He learns how to read it and sing it and say it. He starts to learn as early as age twelve, and the learning goes on for up to ten more years. When he is ready, around age twenty-two, he will get a letter from his main teacher saying that he is a Hindu priest.

Hindu priests lead prayers and teach the Sanskrit holy books, and they know astrology, which is a big deal in Hinduism. *Astrology* is trying to figure out the future by looking at what the planets and stars are doing today. Hindu priests are very close to the people; they help them and marry them and plan cremations for them. Women cannot become Hindu priests.

Yogis are Hindu mystics. To be a Yogi you must also be a Hindu. The Sanskrit word *Yogin* means "one who is becoming one with God." (There is also another Yogi who played catcher, but he was not a Hindu. He was from St. Louis, and he played for the Yankees.) Yogis live in special places called *ashrams.* At the ashram the Hindu will learn from a special teacher called a *guru.* Gurus used to take people away from all cities and all work and all other people to teach them how to get *moksha,* or freedom from the world. Nowadays many gurus teach people to stay in the cities and in the world of other people to get moksha and to help other people get there too.

Breathing is one big way that Yogis learn to be closer to God. Breathing comes naturally to most folks, but the breathing learned by the Yogis is very deep and filled with prayer and love. This kind of breathing is like meditation. It clears the mind to learn the truth and gain moksha. Becoming a Yogi means learning how to control everything about your body and your soul. Yoga is a high and mysterious teaching that reminds us that it is natural to be one with God, as natural as breathing.

CHAPTER 13

How Do You Build a House for God?

—

Building a house for God is not easy. God is huge, so you might want to make the house enormous. But then you remember that God is also inside every one of us, so you also want to make God's house cozy and small. God made every beautiful thing in the world, so you might want to put beautiful things in God's house. Then you remember that God also made very simple things, so you should also fill God's house with simple things. Building a house for God is not easy.

When you look around, you will quickly learn that the religions of the world have done a pretty good job building houses for God. Some are wide and some are narrow, some are grand and some are simple, some are tall and some are small. Every house of God teaches us about God and teaches us about the people who built the house for God. What you believe can be written in a book, *or* it can be written in wood and stone and stained glass. Great houses of God are like songs to God without the music and like poems for God without the words.

A house of God has to do three things: It has to be a good place for people to pray. It has to be a good place for people to study and learn about God and their religion. And it has to be a good place to celebrate the holy times.

Synagogue

A Jewish house of God is called a *synagogue*. Every synagogue has at least two parts. There is the part where Jews come together to pray and read the Torah, called the *beit kenesset*. Then there is the place where children and adults study to learn more about Judaism. That part of the synagogue is called the *beit midrash*.

The place where Jews pray can be built in many different ways, but all the prayer rooms have to have a place called the *aron hakodesh*, or holy ark, to put the Torah scrolls. The ark is at the front of the prayer room, and the prayer room is supposed to be facing Jerusalem, but that does not always happen. For example, in Brooklyn, where all the houses are smushed together real close, you just can't turn the building to face east. When you are praying and you have to choose between facing east and facing the Torah, you always face the Torah.

Orthodox synagogues look a little different from the synagogues of Reform Judaism or Conservative Judaism or Reconstructionist Judaism. The big difference between Orthodox synagogues and other synagogues is that Orthodox synagogues have a divider to keep the men apart from the women during prayer times. This divider is called a *mehitzah*. Sometimes the mehitzah makes the men sit in front and the women in back. Sometimes the women sit in the balcony seats and the men sit on the main floor. Sometimes the men sit on one side and the women sit on the other side.

The idea of separating men and women in prayer happens in

Islam also. Men and women are supposed to think about God, not about each other, and some people think that a divider makes that easier. We know that one of the big reasons why the non-Orthodox parts of Judaism got started was so that men and women could sit together in prayer and so that women could lead the prayer services and do all the things in Judaism that men could always do. The times they are a-changin', but they are not changin' everywhere.

Above the ark, which holds the Torah scrolls, there is a light. Sometimes it is a candle in a holder, and sometimes it is a small electric light. It is in every synagogue, and it is called the *ner tamid,* which means the "eternal light." Of course it isn't really an eternal light. That would mean that it would be on always and forever. If it is a candle, it will burn out, and if it is an electric light, it is going to go out just like your TV goes off in a storm when the power goes out in your neighborhood. So, it is a *sort of* eternal light, and it's a reminder of the light in the Temple in Jerusalem, which the Bible says was kept burning all day and night. The idea of the light is that God is with us always and forever and ever, which, when you think of it, is a very long time.

Church

Lots of churches look like crosses. Some churches have one long hall and then another shorter hall that crosses it, and some don't. The long hall is called the *nave,* which is the Greek word for "boat." The hall that crosses the nave is called the *transept.* The place where the nave and the transept meet—or, if there is no transept, the east end of the nave—is where the altar is, if there is an altar. Some Protestant churches do not have an altar. The altar is the place where the priest stands and says the prayers and the Mass.

In most churches there is also a place for an organ and a choir and a choir leader and also a place for a person to read from the Bible and lead prayers. There is also a place called the *pulpit*, for the priest or minister to give a sermon.

In churches that have altars, there is almost always a cross or a crucifix on or above the altar. A crucifix is a cross with a model of the body of Jesus on it. Some crosses have the body of Jesus wearing a long robe and sort of floating above the cross, not nailed onto the cross. This is called a *Christus Rex* cross, and it is supposed to remind people of the time Jesus rose from the dead.

In Catholic, Orthodox, and many Episcopal churches there are also *tabernacles*. Tabernacles are small places where the bread that has been blessed by the priest can be stored. If there is blessed bread in the tabernacle, there is a light on somewhere near the tabernacle.

Many churches also have *baptismal fonts*, where people are baptized. They look kind of like birdbaths, or little baby swimming pools. All Catholic, some Episcopal, and some Lutheran churches have fourteen pictures around the sides of the church. Each picture has a number. These are called *the stations of the cross*, and they are a way of remembering the story of how Jesus died and rose from the dead. In Lent, the time before Easter, many Christians will walk around all fourteen stations of the cross and stop at each one to remember the great story of Jesus Christ.

Many churches and synagogues have stained-glass windows so that when the light comes in, it becomes all colored and beautiful. In churches the stained-glass windows often have pictures of Jesus or the saints in them. In synagogues they might have pictures of the Torah or the Ten Commandments in them. Stained-glass windows help tell the stories of the religion in a beautiful way.

In Orthodox churches there is a screen or wall with two doors in it between the altar and the nave so that the people can't see what the priest is doing when he is at the altar. This screen is called the *iconostasis*, which means "the screen where the icons are hung." Icons are holy pictures that are very special to Orthodox Christians and help them to pray.

Masjid

A masjid also has two parts. It has an outside place to wash before prayer, and it has a big room for prayer. Lots of times that big room has beautiful carpets on the floor, but it has no furniture in it. Having no seats in the prayer room is a big difference between the way Muslims pray and the way Jews and most Christians pray. Sitting means that you have to have chairs or long benches called *pews*. If you are getting down on your knees and bowing in prayer, which is how Muslims pray, then seats are a huge pain. Hindus have no seats in their temples, and neither do Buddhists. Even some Orthodox Christian churches have no seats in them.

In every masjid there is a little round niche on one wall called the *mihrab*, which shows the direction of Mecca. To the right of the mihrab, there is a pulpit where the imam stands to preach a sermon, called the *khutba*, on Friday at noon, when all Muslims come together to pray.

In masjids, and in many synagogues, you won't find any pictures of people. This is because many Jews and Muslims believe that making pictures of saints or prophets or teachers goes against the second of the Ten Commandments, which says worshiping idols is wrong. They believe that any picture of a person or an animal might become an idol that people would worship instead of God, so they don't put any pictures of anything in the house of prayer. In a masjid you will find words from the Quran in Arabic all around the sides and top of the masjid, or maybe a geometric design, but no pictures!

Many masjids, and all of the big ones, have a tall tower called a *minaret*, which is the place where the *muezzin*, a special person who calls the people to prayer, makes his calls. You can often see the round dome over the prayer room and the tall tower of the minaret from miles away. They are very beautiful shapes, and they tell you that a masjid is there. In the great masjid in Mecca, there are seven minarets; everywhere else, the most you can have is four.

Hindu Temple

When you walk into a Hindu temple, the first thing you see is a big statue of the god who is the main god of that temple. Around that statue are statues of other gods. There is also a place to bring food to the god. The statue of the god is in a big room—which has a tower over it—in the middle of the temple. There is also a smaller room for the prayers, called a *puja*, and this room too has a tower over it. The whole thing is surrounded by a yard with beautiful towers and gardens, and a big wall encloses the whole temple. There is a big bathtub in most Hindu temples, because Hindus have to bathe their whole body before prayer. There is also a tower over the bathing tank.

Buddhist Stupa, Dagoba, and Pagoda

There are three kinds of Buddhist holy places. First there is the *stupa*, a mound of stone and earth that covers a relic and looks like a big gumdrop. A relic is a piece of the Buddha or a piece of the Buddha's clothes. Most of the parts of the Buddha were divided up into eight stupas in India. If the stupa has a watchtower

over it, it is called a *pagoda*. In China pagodas are called *t'a*. The t'a in China can be almost 200 feet tall, with lots of towers on them. They are made in an eight-sided shape because of the eight big teachings of Buddhism. Sometimes they are made out of red bricks.

The Golden Pagoda in Yangon, Myanmar, is called *Shway Dagon*. It has eight hairs in it that Buddhists say are hairs from the Buddha. This pagoda also has a pointed dome over it that is covered in pure gold! It is the place where Buddhists from all over southeast Asia come on a pilgrimage, just like Muslims make a pilgrimage to Mecca.

CHAPTER 14

Can I Talk to God?

Talking is not nearly as important as listening. When you talk, all you hear is your own voice. When you listen, you may hear something that can make you wise. All religions teach us to listen.

Religions that believe in God teach people to listen to God. It is not that hard to hear God; it is just hard to believe that what you are hearing really is from God. We hear God when that voice inside of us says, "Don't steal that candy bar!" or "Don't punch Herbie in the nose!" That inside voice is called our conscience, but it is really the voice of God speaking to us to help us be better people.

We also hear God when we hear the waves crash against the shore or the birds singing in the trees. God has many voices, and we have many ears. Listening is a good thing, a very good thing. Almost everybody who gets good at talking to God starts out by getting good at listening to God.

Talking to God is called *praying,* and what you say to God is called a *prayer*. Some of the prayers you say to God have never been said before by anyone. These are personal prayers. Personal prayers come from your soul, hit your lips on the way out, and go straight on to God.

Other prayers have the same words in them each and every time you say them. These are communal prayers. Communal prayers are the prayers that have been written down in the prayer book of a religion. All religions that believe in God have communal prayers in them. Even the religions that do not believe in God and those that believe in many gods have chants and meditations that do just what prayers do.

The reason all religions have prayers or chants or meditations is that all human beings need to say four things in their lives. Those four things that all people need to say are: Thanks!, Wow!, Gimme!, and Oops! Let's look at them.

Thanks! Prayers

Saying thank you is a good idea when you talk to people, and it is a very good idea when you are talking to God. Thank-you prayers are the way we say, "God, I know that I did not really deserve all the good things that have happened to me. I know that You are the reason all good things come into the world, and so I just wanted to say Thank You! for this good thing that has happened to me and for all the good things that happen to me day after day. I may not always say it, but I always mean it. Thank You!"

Muslims teach that if we say thank you to Allah for the simple things in life, we will never forget to say thank you to Allah for the big things. The Quran teaches, "It is God who made the night for you, that you may rest therein, and the day, as that which helps you to see. It is true that God is full of grace and bounty to people, but most people give no thanks."

Buddhist Thanks! prayers are not addressed to God, because they don't believe in God. They are addressed instead to the Buddha. One of the ways that Buddhists teach us to give thanks is by reminding us that we can never give enough thanks for all that the Buddha has done for us. This is from the Lotus Sutra: "You the World Honored One [the Buddha] are a great giver of things. You taught us and helped us because of your love for us. No one will be able to repay your favors even if he tries to do it for many hundreds of millions of kalpas [a kalpa is a very, very long time]. No one will be able to repay your favors even if he bows to you in respect and offers you his hands or feet or anything else. No one will be able to repay your favors even if he carries you on his head or shoulders and respects you from the bottom of his heart for as many kalpas as there are sands in the River Ganges."

Not saying thank you is kind of like stealing something good from God. That is the lesson of a teaching from the Yoruba tribe in Africa: "One who has received kindness but will not say thank you is worse than a robber who carries away our belongings."

Christianity teaches that Jesus offers a way for us to give thanks to God. In fact, Jesus is the biggest reason to give thanks in Christianity. This teaching is from Saint Paul: "Whatever you do, in word or deed, do everything in the name of the Lord Jesus, giving thanks to God the Father through him."

The Jews have a thank-you prayer for all happy times: "You are Blessed, O Lord our God, who has kept us alive and sustained us and enabled us to reach this happy time." But Judaism teaches that we must say thank-you prayers not just at the good times but at all times. The rabbis taught, "Do not be like those people who honor their gods when things are going good for them and curse their gods when things go bad. In pleasure or in pain, give thanks!"

Wow! Prayers

Wow! prayers are prayers about things that really have nothing to do with blessings that have been given to each of us alone. Wow! prayers are about blessings that have been given to the whole world. Wow! prayers are the prayers we say when we run across something beautiful or wonderful or powerful in the world.

When we see a rainbow, we should say a Wow! prayer, or when we hear thunder or see a butterfly or the big waves of the ocean. Wow! prayers are the way we say to God, "This thing I just saw or felt or smelled is terrific and beautiful, wonderful and awesome. I am saying this prayer so You know that I know that You know that I know that You had something to do with this. Keep up the good work!"

Hindus have a sound that they use when they say a Wow! prayer. It is the sound that they believe comes from the soul of the whole universe. That sound is *Ommmmmmm!* and they say Ommmmmmm! when they are meditating to help them feel the sound of the universe inside them. The Hindus have many prayers that start with Ommmmmmm! Here is a great one from the Rig-Veda: "Ommmmmmm! We meditate upon the glorious splendor of the Holy One who makes Life and who is a god. May he himself make our minds bright. Ommmmmmm!"

Jews have lots of Wow! prayers. They all start out with the words "You are Blessed, O Lord our God, King of the Universe...," and then you fill in what the King of the Universe has done. If you just heard thunder, you say the beginning words and end with "... whose mighty power fills the world." If you just saw the ocean, you finish with the words "... who has made the great sea." If it is a rainbow, you remember the Bible story that God made the rainbow after Noah and the flood to show that the world would never be flooded out again and you say, "... who remembers the promise to Noah and who keeps all promises."

Feeling the wonder of the earth and heaven and all the life and blessings that tie them together is the reason we say Wow! If you go through life and never say Wow!, you better slow down or speed up or do something to get yourself to see all the Wow! that is in heaven and the earth all around you.

This feeling of Wow! prayers is in Psalm 8, which King David wrote to be sung with a harp: "O Lord, our Lord, how majestic is Your name in all the earth. You have covered the heavens with Your splendor." We also learn the Wow! feeling about nature from the religions of the Native Americans. A Round Dance Song from the Cree people has these words: "The Sky blesses me, the Earth blesses me; Up in the Skies I cause to dance the Spirits; On the Earth, the people I cause to dance."

Wow! prayers help us to stay in awe of nature. If we can still say Wow! about the things we see in the world, we will take better care of the world. Religions help us to see the Wow! in the world, and there is a lot of Wow! out there.

Gimme! Prayers

When most people think of prayer, they are thinking of the Gimme! prayers. These are the prayers in which we ask God to give us something or not to take away something that we already have. There is nothing wrong with Gimme! prayers if the things we are asking God to give us are good things. But if the things are silly things or stupid things or things that we should get for ourselves, then Gimme! prayers can be silly and stupid too.

Sports can bring out some pretty stupid Gimme! prayers, like when golfers pray to make a putt or when basketball players pray to make the basket. There is nothing wrong with praying for strength or courage to face a loss or for the grace to be a good winner, but asking God to help you win a game is not worthy of the friendship, trust, and love we should have for God and God always has for us. It is like begging God to make you rich.

Here are some great Gimme! prayers from the religions of the world. These are all prayers that ask for things from God, but they ask for things in a humble way, and they ask for good things, not stupid things. The first is the Lord's Prayer, from the Gospel of Matthew.

> Our Father who art in heaven,
> Hallowed be thy Name.
> Thy kingdom come,
> Thy will be done,
> On earth as it is in heaven.
> Give us this day our daily bread;
> And forgive us our debts,
> As we also have forgiven our debtors;
> And lead us not into temptation,
> But deliver us from evil.

There is a prayer from the Nuder tribe in Sudan, in Africa, that is kind of like the Lord's Prayer.

> Our Father, it is thy universe, it is thy will,
> Let us be at peace, let the souls of the people be cool.
> Thou art our Father; remove all evil from our path.

Here is the priests' blessing from the Book of Numbers, in the Hebrew Bible:

May the Lord bless you and keep you,
May the Lord make His face to shine upon you and be
    gracious to you;
May the Lord lift up His face to you and give you peace.

This prayer is from the Upanishads of Hinduism:

From the unreal lead me to the Real!
From darkness lead me to the light!
From death lead me to immortality!
Ommmmmmm.

From the Quran we learn this prayer:

Our Lord! Lo! We have heard a crier calling unto faith, "Believe in your Lord!" So we believed. Our Lord! Therefore forgive us our sins, and take from us our evil deeds, and make us die the death of the righteous.

These are all great Gimme! prayers because they ask for good things that we sometimes really can't get for ourselves. They ask for hope and forgiveness, for courage and protection, for wisdom and peace.

Oops! Prayers

Saying "I'm sorry" is one of the hardest things for some people to say. Some people must think that they are perfect and that they never do anything wrong, never hurt somebody else's feelings, never forget to do something important, and never mess up. One of the main reasons to talk to God in prayer is to help us learn how to say that we are sorry. Saying we are sorry in a prayer makes us remember that we messed up. Most Oops! prayers make us say the bad thing we did right in the prayer so we can't dodge it. The Oops! prayers also remind us of the teachings of our religion about doing the right thing and help us to get a clear idea of how we should act better the next time. Maybe the most important thing that Oops! prayers do is to help us get up the guts to face the people we have hurt and ask them to forgive us.

When you say what you did, when you see how wrong it was, and when you try to patch up things with the people you have hurt, your life gets better. Making your life better is a very hard thing to try to do, but making your life better is the very best thing you can try to do. Religions help you do it, and that is one of the big reasons why religions will always be around.

One great Oops! prayer comes from Judaism. Jews have a holy fast day called Yom Kippur in which Jews spend the whole day saying Oops! prayers, not eating or drinking anything, and trying to patch up things with God and with each other. When it comes time to say the Oops! prayer, everybody in the synagogue stands up and recites a long list of sins that all start out, "For the sin we have sinned against You, God, by . . ." The list includes sins done in secret and sins done in front of people, sins of not respecting parents and teachers, sins of cheating, sins of making people do what we want just because we have power over them, sins of gossip and sins of swearing, sins of anger and sins of jealousy, sins of hitting and sins of thinking about hitting. After the long list everybody says, "For all these sins, O God of mercy, forgive us, pardon us, grant us atonement!"

Christians also have lots of Oops! prayers; they are said at the beginning of almost every prayer service. Catholics say an Oops!

prayer at the beginning of the Mass. They also have a special Oops! prayer called the Act of Contrition that goes like this: "My God, I am sorry for my sins with all my heart. In choosing to do wrong and failing to do good, I have sinned against You whom I should love above all things. I firmly intend, with Your help, to do penance, to sin no more, and to avoid whatever leads me to sin. Jesus Christ suffered and died for us. In his name, dear God, forgive me. Amen."

Muslims pray to Allah five times a day, and there is an Oops! prayer in there each time! It is called the supplication for forgiveness (two big words and one little word that come together to just mean Oops!). The prayer is, "O Allah, forgive me and forgive my parents. Please bless them as they have raised me from when I was an infant. O Allah, I have been greatly unjust to myself and none grant protection against faults but You. Please protect me with a protection that comes from You. Have mercy on me. You are the Forgiving One, the Merciful One."

There is a Tibetan Buddhist Oops! prayer that goes like this: "In this life which has no beginning and no end; in this life or in other lives, because of my ignorance, I have done many wrongs. I also told others to do wrong and I have been happy when they did wrong. Now that I understand my faults, I confess them to the Protectors from my heart. I join my palms asking the buddhas of all directions, 'Please light the lamp of the teaching for beings who suffer in dark confusion.'"

Hindus learn this Oops! prayer from the Rig-Veda: "What then O Varuna is my greatest sin? Tell me, O God who knows all and lacks nothing, so that I can quickly bow down and ask pardon. Set us free from the yoke of the sins of our fathers, and also from the sins we have done ourselves. Release your servant as a thief is set free from his crime or as a calf is set free from the leash."

Some Ways of Praying

The religions of the world have lots of different ways of saying their communal prayers. Here are some of the big differences in how the religions pray.

There are some prayers you have to say with your shoes off and some prayers you can say with your shoes on.

In some of the religions in the world you pray with your shoes on, and in some you pray with your shoes off. This may seem to be a silly difference, but maybe not. Muslims pray with no shoes on because they believe shoes are kind of an insult to God because shoes say, "I want to get out of here as soon as I can."

There are some prayers you have to say in a group and some prayers you can say alone.

All religions let you pray alone when you are saying personal prayers, but some religions make you pray in a group when you are saying communal prayers. In Judaism you need ten men to pray the communal prayers. This group of ten men over the age of thirteen is called a *minyan*. In non-Orthodox Judaism, women can be counted in a minyan, but all parts of Judaism need a minyan to pray together three times a day. Actually, the second and the third prayer times are usually put together, so it is really just twice a day—once in the morning and once in the evening—that Jews are supposed to pray.

Hinduism teaches that you have to pray three times a day. Their three times are before the sun comes up, after the sun comes up, and at night. The Hindu takes a bath before prayer times, which is not that hard because most Hindus pray at home. Hindus also put out food for the gods. If they enter a temple, they bow down to the ground until they touch their forehead. And they always back out of the temple so that they never turn their backs to the god of that temple.

Muslims pray five times a day, alone or in a group. The prayers are called *salat.*

Bowing happens in a lot of prayer services. It is a sign that we are nothing compared to God. Many Christians bow in front of the altar. Jews bow in front of the ark that holds the Torah scrolls.

Muslims bow facing the Kabah in the city of Mecca. They bow, like Hindus, with their forehead touching the ground. Each time of prayer for Muslims has a set number of bows in it: three bows after sunset, four bows at night, two bows at dawn, four at noon, and four in the afternoon.

Muslim prayers start with the bows. The people stand in straight rows behind the *imam,* the person leading them in prayer. He speaks first, and they repeat what he says in a soft voice. In every prayer service a Muslim says, *"Allahu akbar,"* which means "God is great." They also say the first words of the Quran. At the end of the prayer service, each person says, *"as-salamu alai-kum,"* which means "peace be upon you." The ways the Muslim bows in prayer include touching the nose to the ground, sitting back on the heels, kneeling, and other movements. Orthodox Jews rock back and forth and bow a lot during prayers too. They call it *davening.* Many religions understand that bowing is a way to help prayers come from our whole body, not just our lips.

Reading the Holy Books—Listening to Scripture

Almost all religions include parts of the holy books in the prayer service. This is a good way to teach the holy books to the people when they come together for prayer. Jews read from the Torah in every Sabbath prayer service. Christians read from the Hebrew Bible and the New Testament, and Hindus read from the

Vedas. Buddhists read from the Sutta, which are the stories of the Buddha. Prayer services are really times for teaching the holy book as much as they are times for asking God for stuff.

When Christians meet as a group to pray on Sundays, they listen to some readings from the Bible. They sing some songs that are called hymns, and they listen to a sermon. A *sermon* is a talk that the priest or minister gives to teach the people what the Bible readings mean and what Jesus would do if Jesus were here now. Sermons are in the prayer services of many religions. Sermons can be very powerful and very sad and very happy. Sermons can sometimes be real boring, but none of the sermons we give are like that!

There are some prayers only a priest can say and some prayers anybody can say.

There are two things that only a priest can do. Only a priest can hear *confession,* which is when a priest listens while the person tells the priest all the sinful things he or she did. The priest forgives them for their sins and then tells them how to go out and fix up what they did that was wrong.

The other thing only a priest can do is say the Mass, sometimes called celebrating the Mass. The Mass is the way Christians act out the last supper Jesus had on earth. Eating the bread and drinking the wine is the way Christians get so close to Jesus that they feel Jesus inside them. Eating the bread and drinking the wine helps them to remember what Jesus did and how he lived. The Mass is really a great group prayer. Eating the bread and drinking the wine is called taking Communion or Eucharist.

Most all Christians take Communion. Catholics and some Episcopalians take Communion every Sunday, and they could take it every day. Some Lutherans and some Orthodox Christians take Communion every week, and some take it only at holiday times and at a few other special Sundays during the year. Some Protestants—including Baptists, Methodists, Presbyterians, and Evangelicals—rarely take Communion.

In Shinto, the religion of Japan, there are lots of prayers that only a Shinto priest can say. Some of these prayers are done in front of shrines or altars, and they are kind of like messages to relatives who have died. These prayers are called *norito*.

In Buddhism and Hinduism there are also prayers that can be said only by the priests. Some of these prayers are like Shinto prayers to the dead. The Buddhist monks have a really neat way of praying that only they can do. They have a kind of prayer machine, called a Buddhist prayer wheel. The words of the prayer are put on the wheel, and it is spun around. The teaching is that each time the wheel goes around once, the prayer is said once. This means that you can get your prayer said millions of times without getting hoarse.

CHAPTER 15

Why Does Bad Stuff Happen to Good Folks?

For most folks the hardest question about religion is: How can bad stuff happen to good folks? Good stuff is supposed to happen to good folks and bad stuff is supposed to happen to bad folks, but the world doesn't always work out that way. There are times when good folks lose their jobs and bad folks get good jobs, when good folks get sick and die, while bad folks have great health and die at a ripe old age. There is a lot in the world that is just not fair! Islam, Christianity, and Judaism teach that God is very good and very powerful, but if God is so good why is there so much bad?

Let's look at what the religions have to say about the bad stuff.

"The Bad Stuff Is Our Fault."

Even though not all the religions in the world believe in God, all the religions in the world do believe that a lot of the bad stuff that happens to us is our own fault. You may have heard people say, "What goes around comes around." This means that what we do comes back to us. If we do bad things, bad things come back to us. If we do good things, good things come back to us. This does not happen all the time, but it happens lots of times. If you lie, people won't believe you. If you cheat, people won't trust you. If you are cruel to people, people won't love you. What goes around comes around.

Many religions teach that some of the ways people die are just plain and simple their own fault. People smoke and die of lung cancer. People use drugs and die of overdoses. People eat food full of fat and sugar, then don't exercise, and die of heart attacks. People drive too fast and die in car crashes. It is sad when anybody dies, but it is very sad when people die because of things they do to themselves. That is why there are good reasons to believe the teachings of the religions that a lot of the bad stuff that happens to us is our fault.

Now, this does not mean that *all* the bad stuff that happens to us is our fault. It only means that the way many religions see things, lots of bad stuff that does happen to us is our fault. How much is our fault and how much is bad luck is one of the big questions that will never go away. Let's look at another idea.

"The Bad Stuff Is Nobody's Fault."

Even though lots of bad stuff that happens to us is our fault, not *all* the bad stuff that happens can be our fault. The babies who die did nothing wrong. The people who get hurt in accidents caused by other people did nothing wrong. The people who die from many types of cancer or AIDS that have nothing to do with what they ate or smoked or how they lived—these people got sick, and they did nothing wrong.

There is something about the world that makes some bad

stuff happen. This something is what makes life on planet earth full of suffering. For Buddhists the suffering in the world is called *dukka.* Knowing that the world is full of suffering is the first of the Four Noble Truths of Buddhism. For Buddhists the bad stuff in the world happens because of the way the world is. The world and everything in it comes into being, gets old and broken, and dies. That is the way of the world for everything, and this way makes us sad. That sadness is the reason for suffering. The only way to get rid of the bad stuff is to not care so much about the world and in that way get free of the world.

Jews have a way of teaching that some of the bad stuff in the world is not our fault. They teach *olam k'minhago noheg,* which sort of means, "The world goes along just the way it goes and some bad stuff happens just because of the way the world is and not because you did something wrong."

Another way to think of this is to think that the world has holes in it. The holes are the things in the world that are not fixed yet. God put these holes in the world so that we would have something to figure out and fix. If you were God and You made people with huge brains and lots of free time, You might want people to use their brains to patch up the holes in the world. The holes are things like diseases we haven't cured and floods that wash our town away and droughts that dry up our crops. Or the way you can get a zit on the end of your nose just before you are going out on a big date, and the way the person on the other end of the phone hangs up just as you pick up. These are just some of the very big and very little holes in the world that God put there for us to patch. The holes are not our fault, but if we don't care enough to try and patch the holes, *that* is our fault.

Knowing that some bad stuff is not our fault is important. It is hard enough to be sick. If somebody comes along and tells you

that you got sick because of some bad thing you did, that makes being sick even harder to take. This is why some religions teach that the bad stuff is not our fault. The important thing is to know the difference between things that are our fault and things that are not our fault.

"The Bad Stuff Is the Devil's Fault."

Another way religions teach that the bad stuff is not our fault says that the bad stuff comes from the devil or bad spirits or bad gods who want to hurt us. All kids know about boogey monsters. Boogey monsters are the monsters kids think live in our closets and under our beds and in the basement and in dark hallways and in the forest. Some religions teach that boogey monsters are *real*.

Religions have lots of names for the chief boogey monster or the bad god. In Judaism and Christianity he is called Satan, Lucifer, or Beelzebub. In Zoroastrianism, it is Angra Mainyu. The Dinka, an African tribe living in Sudan, call him Macardit. Hindus call him Shiva.

One of the important things to remember about the boogey monster or the bad god is that every religion that teaches that bad is real also teaches that the good is really much stronger than the bad. What this means is that you have nothing to be afraid of if you live a good life.

One final thing to say about the bad stuff that is our fault and the bad stuff that isn't: We need courage to admit when we do something wrong. Nowadays many people who do bad things try to blame everybody else for what they did. This does not wash. Some bad stuff happens because of us, and some doesn't. Isn't it better to know the difference?

CHAPTER 16

How Should We Live?

You should know by now that not all the religions believe in God, and not all the religions that believe in God believe in *one* God. But every religion teaches us how to live the right way. Along with teaching us not to freak out about death, teaching us our place in the world, and teaching us how to pray, teaching us the right way to live is one of the four things *all* the religions of the world do.

The teachings of all the religions about the right way to live are almost exactly the same. The reason for this is that all the religions know a big thing, and that is: How we act is more important than what we believe! Of course believing the right thing and then doing the right thing is best of all, but if somebody believes all the right things and then doesn't do them, that person is not as good as somebody who does the right things even if they don't know why. *Doing* is much more important to religions than believing.

Here is a list of some of the things that all the religions of the world have taught us to do.

Do to Other People What You Want Them to Do to You

This is sometimes called the "golden rule," and it pops up in almost the same words in nearly every religion. This rule really works, because it teaches us that if we just stop and think about how we want to be treated, we will know right away just exactly how to treat other people: Treat them the same way we want to be treated ourselves.

It is amazing just how many religions have some form of the golden rule. In the Talmud of Judaism we read, "The things you hate should not be done to others." In the New Testament of Christianity, in the Gospel of Luke, chapter six, we are taught, "Do to others what you would wish them to do to you." In Buddhism, in the book called the Udanavarga, we see it again: "Do not hurt others in ways that would hurt you." Hinduism has the golden rule too. In the Mahabharata it is put this way: "Do nothing to others that would cause you pain if they did it to you." Islam teaches in the Sunan: "You are not a real Muslim until you want for other people what you want for yourself." The Analects of Confucius in China has this: "Do nothing to others that you would not want them to do to you."

Every religion has some way to teach us that what we like, we should do to others, and what we don't like, we shouldn't do to others. Life can be real complicated, but if you follow the golden rule, it gets a lot simpler and a lot better.

Respect All Living Things

The reason that Judaism and Christianity and Islam give for respecting all living things is simple: God made them, so we should respect them. We see this taught in the 24th Psalm: "The earth is the Lord's and the fulness thereof, the world and those who dwell therein."

We also see this same reason in a song of the Ashanti tribe in Ghana and the Ivory Coast of Africa:

The stream crosses the path, the path crosses the stream:
Which of them is older?
Did we not cut the path to go and meet this stream?
The stream was born long, long ago.
It was born because of the Creator
who created things pure, pure.

We also hear this in a Shinto teaching: "Even in a single leaf of a tree or in a little blade of grass, the awe-inspiring God is manifest." And we learn in the Oracle of Atsuta from the Shinto religion, "All of you under heaven! Think of heaven as your father, earth as your mother, and all things as your brothers and sisters."

Some religions teach that it is wrong to kill living things even if it seems like you have to. The Jains of India believe that, and so do most Buddhists and Hindus. This teaching that it is *always* wrong to hurt or kill anything is called *ahimsa*. It means absolute nonviolence. The Jains go everywhere with a broom and sweep the road in front of them so that they will not even step on a bug! The Jains teach it this way: "The essence of right conduct is not to injure anyone; one should know only this, that noninjury is religion." They also teach, "As a mother with her own life guards the life of her own child, may you have thoughts to guard all the living things in the world." And, "One should not injure, subjugate, enslave, torture, or kill any animal, living being, organism, or sentient being. This doctrine of nonviolence is immaculate, immutable, and eternal. Just as suffering is painful to you, in the same way it is painful, disquieting, and terrifying to all animals, living beings, organisms, and sentient beings."

All the religions in the world teach us to respect life, and one of the main ways to respect life is not to take a life. The reason is like this: You are not God; only God can give life, so only God can take life away. The Bible teaches this in the sixth of the Ten Commandments, "Thou shalt not murder." There is even a good story from the Talmud that teaches us how important each person's life is to God: "God made only one person to begin all life. He was named Adam. The reason for this is to teach us that anyone who takes a single life is like a person who has killed all life in the world, and one who saves a single life is like one who has saved all the life of the world."

The Hindus teach it in the Laws of Manu: "A person who murders is more wicked than a defamer, more wicked than a thief, and more wicked than somebody who injures a person with a stick."

In the Quran we learn that murders are hated even by God: "Anyone who kills a person will have his reward in hell and will stay there forever. God will be angry with him and curse him and prepare bad things for him."

So, one of the main things that all the religions in the world teach us is to respect life, and one of the main ways of doing that is not to kill. But the difference is that some religions will let you kill *sometimes.* Here are the times.

You Can Kill Animals for Food

The vegetarian religions, like Buddhism, do not let you kill animals, but Judaism and Christianity and Islam let you kill animals *if* you are going to eat them or if somebody else is going to eat them. The idea of going into the forest with a big gun and blowing animals away for no reason except that you like doing it is against all the teachings of all the religions. Many hunters are learning this. If they are not going to eat it, they should not kill it. Many people who like to fish are now letting fish go after they catch them, if they are not going to eat them.

We think that the vegetarians, the people who don't eat meat, have a real good point. If you can live without killing some living thing for lunch, it seems to us like a good way to live. We think we should all try to live our lives so that the fewest number of living things have to die because we want lunch. Maybe we should remember the teaching of the Yoruba tribe from Nigeria, in Africa, who teach their children, "If you are going to take a pointed stick to spear a baby bird, you should first spear yourself to feel how it hurts."

Even the religions that teach that it is okay to kill animals for food also teach that we should be *very* respectful of the animals we do kill for food. The Bible teaches that when we collect eggs from a nest to make breakfast, we should scare away the mother bird so that she does not have to see somebody take her eggs. Confucius never fished with a net but only with one line and one hook so he would not kill too many fish. The Sioux tribe of the Native Americans hunted buffalo in the old days, and they would say this prayer whenever they killed a buffalo: "Look at this buffalo, O Grandfather, which you have given us. He is the chief of all four-legged animals who walk upon our Sacred

Mother Earth. From him the people live and with him we walk the sacred path."

By the way, respecting animals' lives also means that we should drive carefully so that we don't squash squirrels and raccoons and possums and deer as we speed down the highways of life.

You Can Kill a Person Who Is Trying to Kill You

There is just too much killing of people by other people. *Way too much killing!* Religions all teach us not to kill each other. But if somebody is trying to kill you or your family and you can't run away, and you have no other choice, then some religions say it is okay to kill that person before he or she kills you. This is called killing in *self-defense.* Many religions say that it is wrong for you to just let somebody else come over and kill you. These religions say that if you can stop it, you should. These religions teach that if you are defending yourself, killing can be the right thing to do.

Judaism, Christianity, and Islam say that killing in self-defense is okay. Jesus taught in the fifth chapter of the Gospel of Matthew: "You have heard that it was said, 'An eye for an eye and a tooth for a tooth.' But I say to you, Do not stand up against an evil person. If somebody slaps you on the right cheek, turn the other cheek. If somebody wants to take your coat, give him your coat and your cape, and if anybody makes you walk a mile, walk two miles with him."

Some Christians read this teaching and say that Jesus did *not* believe in self-defense; God *always* wants us to turn the other cheek, forgive even our worst enemies, and preserve life no matter what. But other Christians think that what Jesus was really saying was that we should do *everything* we can to avoid hurting another person or killing another person, but if we have to kill somebody to save our life, it is okay. Knowing when it's okay and when it isn't okay to kill another person is one of the biggest questions in living life the right way. The problem often is that the question comes up real fast, and we don't have a lot of time to think it over.

Hindus and Buddhists, who don't kill animals for any reason, are *not* going to teach that killing people is okay for any reason. They do not teach that killing in self-defense is the way we are supposed to live. In the Dhammapada of Buddhism we learn, "One should neither strike nor cause others to strike. Life is dear to all, and so one should not strike nor cause to strike. Whoever, seeking his own happiness, harms with the stick will know no happiness in the life after death."

These peaceful teachings remind us of the big problem with teaching that killing in self-defense is okay. If you teach that *some* killing is okay, then you are likely to get a lot of killing that is not okay. Some people can think that they are killing in self-defense, but they are really killing out of anger or jealousy or greed. If you let people kill for *any* reason, it kind of opens up the door for killing people. And that is a hard door to close once you open it.

We see this in wars. Some wars are really like self-defense. In some wars, people are attacked by other people for no reason, and the people who are attacked have to kill the invaders to protect their families and their homes and their land. Judaism, Christianity, and Islam teach that this is okay, but the problem is that some nations fight wars and trick their people into thinking that it is a war of defense when really it is just an attack to steal something somebody else owns.

The Confucians and the Buddhists and the Taoists teach that *all* wars are wrong. Confucius taught, "In wars to gain land, the land is filled with dead bodies. In wars to gain cities, the cities are filled with dead bodies. Those who fight wars should get the worst punishments after they die."

Never fighting in a war does keep you from fighting in a war that is wrong, but never fighting in a war also makes you a sitting duck for some bad person with an army who wants to come in and hurt you and your family and your friends and take your video games and drive your car without permission! It is a tough choice, but all the religions in the world teach us to be *very* careful in making the choice to go to war.

If You See People Who Need Help, You Should Help Them

Helping those who need help is a big teaching of all the religions. The Bible is filled with verses that teach us to take care of the poor and feed the hungry. Psalm 41 says, "Blessed is the one who cares for the poor." The fifteenth chapter of Deuteronomy teaches, "You shall not harden your heart . . . against your poor brother, but you shall open your hand to him . . . because there will always be poor people in the land." Hardening our hearts to the poor happens a lot, especially in big cities. You see so many poor people begging and in trouble that it is hard, very hard, to feel sorry for all of them. So many folks let their hearts get hard. They say, "These folks are just bums. Why don't they go out and get a job?" Saying this makes it a lot easier not to do anything to help them. That is what the Bible means when it says, "Don't harden your heart or shut your hand against your poor brother." It means that no matter how much it hurts to see these poor people lying all over the place, it hurts *more* to be one of them.

The Bible teaches us to take care of the poor because all people are made in the image of God, so helping them is like helping God. Respecting them is like respecting God. Loving them is like loving God. Also, God made the world, and so God owns the world and everything in it. This means that *all* our stuff is really God's stuff, and we are supposed to give some of it away to people who need help, because that is what God wants.

There is a great law in chapter nineteen in the book of Leviticus that teaches that when you plant a field of wheat or a vineyard of grapes and the time comes to harvest them, you can't take all the wheat in your field or all the grapes on your vines. You have to leave some of the wheat in the field and some of the grapes on the vine for poor people to come into your field and pick so that they will have something to eat.

Taking care of the poor is also something that we should all do. The Tract of the Quiet Way, a holy book in Taoism, teaches, "You should help people in trouble right away just like you have to let a fish trapped in a net go free right away or it will die. You have to get people out of danger right away just like you have to free a sparrow from a net right away or it will choke. Be kind to orphans, and help widows. Respect old people and help the poor."

Islam adds to that list, "Be kind to parents, and to your relatives, and to orphans and to the poor and to the neighbor who is your relative, and to the neighbor who is a total stranger, and to your friend, and to the traveler." Seeing how you treat strangers can be a test to see how good you really are. It is no big deal to be kind to somebody you know and love. It's easy to be kind to somebody in your family, unless it's your goofy cousin Herbie who is always asking you for money, but being kind to a total stranger takes a good heart.

In the Quran we learn the story of how Muhammad passed the test with flying colors. A stranger came to see Muhammad at

a time when he had no money and hardly any food. He just had enough food for dinner for his children. He told his wife to put his children to bed with no dinner and give the little food in the house to the stranger. No wonder Muslims love Muhammad.

There is a story like that from Hinduism about a man named Rantiveda, who gave away almost everything he ever made and lived in poverty with his family so that he could give to other people. Once there was no food and only a little water in the house for forty-eight days. Rantiveda was dying of thirst, but just then a beggar came to his place looking for a drink of water. Rantiveda said, "I do not want from God the power of the gods, and I do not want to be free from rebirth. I only want to be a part of the hearts of all people. I take on their suffering that they will be free of misery." Then he gave away the last of his water, and the gods of the three worlds came to him with blessings.

There is a story from Jewish life in Europe some two hundred years ago. The story is about Bonsha Zweig. He was a poor man, but he gave to all the other poor people, just like Muhammad and just like Rantiveda. When he died a poor man, he was welcomed to heaven by God and by all the angels, who offered him any reward for his life of charity. He thought for a minute and then asked if he might have a warm roll with butter. The angels bowed to him, because even in heaven he wanted almost nothing.

A Winnebago Indian wrote down his advice to his children: "See to it that whoever enters your house gets something to eat, even if you hardly have anything." The Gospel of Luke in the third chapter teaches, "He who has two coats, let him share with him who has none; and he who has food, let him do the same." In the New Testament letter to the Hebrews, we read, "Always be kind to strangers, for in being kind to strangers, some people have entertained angels unawares." This means that the stranger you are helping might really be an angel. You just never know!

Islam has a wonderful way of teaching charity: "Every joint in a person's body should perform a charity every day: to act justly between two people is a charity; to help a person get onto a horse is a charity; a good word is a charity; every step you take to go to pray is a charity; and removing something dangerous from the road is a charity."

Rabbi Moses Maimonides, who lived in Spain and Egypt about 800 years ago, taught that Judaism believed in thirteen levels of charity. The lowest level is not even to give enough and only to give after people ask you again and again. The highest level is to help a person find a job so that they will not need to take charity from anybody ever again.

Now, you might think, "Why do we need to be taught to help people? Don't people help other people without being taught to do it?" The answer is No! If people are not taught by religions to help each other, they will see that it is easier to steal from the weak than help the weak. Teaching us to help other people is one of the ways religions help us to learn to care about people more than stuff.

Helping others is also one of the ways religions teach us to be different from the animals. Lions chase the weakest antelopes and wolves chase the weakest deer. In nature the strongest survive and the weakest die. That is the way of the world in nature, which is a world where there is no religion. But human beings who have religion have learned that it is better and right to help the weak.

When you help others, do not do it because you want some reward. The Quran teaches: "You should feed the poor and the orphan and the prisoner, all because of love for Allah, and you should say to the ones you feed, 'I wish no reward. I do not need you to say thank you to me.'" The idea that you do not need people to say thank you and you do not need a reward for helping the poor is another big idea of Judaism, Christianity, and Islam. The Bible teaches that giving is a normal and natural thing for all of us to do. The Bible teaches that charity is not something special that makes us really great. Charity is like breathing or eating. It is a natural and normal part of the way we should live. It's just like candles, only better, because a candle only lights up one room, but charity lights up the whole world.

Play Fair

Justice is another word for playing fair. All the religions teach us that we should work for justice in our world, that we should play fair. Injustice is when some people are treated better than others for no good reason.

The Bible teaches about justice in many ways. For people who do not have justice and freedom, the Bible teaches us to work hard to get them justice and to get them freedom. The prophets in the Bible were very angry when justice was not done. These were the words the prophet Amos heard from God: "I do not want to hear your singing, and I will not listen to your music, until you let justice roll down like waters, and righteousness like an ever-flowing stream." Jeremiah, another prophet, said it this way: "This is the word of the Lord: Do justice and righteousness, and deliver from the hand of the oppressor the one who has been robbed."

The Quran teaches the same thing: "God commands justice and kindness and giving to other people." In another place in the Quran we learn, "Stand for justice as a witness for God . . . even if that means standing against yourself or your parents or your family. Stand for justice even if it means standing against the rich or against the poor, for God protects justice. Do not follow what your heart tells you to do, for that might make you do what is not just." Islam teaches that the only reason for governments is to do justice. "The government is the guardian of those who have no guardian."

Hinduism has this teaching about justice: "There is nothing higher than justice. A weak man can defeat even a strong man through justice. It is like having the help of a king."

Cut People Some Slack

Forgiveness is the word we use for cutting people some slack. It means that if people hurt you or if they don't do what they are supposed to do, and then they understand that what they did was wrong and they say they are sorry, you are supposed to cut them some slack and forgive them. All the religions teach us that we cannot live together unless we learn to forgive each other.

In Islam we learn that "the best deed of a great person is to forgive and forget." In Confucianism we learn in the I Ching, "The great person forgives wrongs and is lenient with crimes." From Taoism we learn, "Show patience even when you are being humiliated and do not bear a grudge." Forgiving people is more important than doing the rituals of a religion. We learn this from the New Testament in the fifth chapter of the Gospel of Matthew: "If you are bringing a gift to the altar, and you remember that your brother has something against you, you should leave your gift right there before the altar and go make peace with your brother and only then come back and offer the gift." In Judaism, the holiday of Yom Kippur is the day Jews pray to God to forgive their sins, but the Talmud teaches that "the Day of Atonement atones for sins which are only against God. For sins against another person, the Day of Atonement does not atone until you have made peace with the person who has been hurt."

The biggest act of forgiveness we have found in the holy books of the religions of the world is the story of how Jesus forgave the Roman soldiers who killed him. When Jesus was crucified, Jesus said, "Father forgive them; for they know not what they do." To forgive the people who killed you is amazing and teaches us all a lesson: We can't ask God to forgive us unless we are ready to forgive others.

CHAPTER 17

What Happens After We Die?

Living is wonderful, but it's not forever.

Everything that lives must die someday, and that has always been a great mystery for people. When we are alive, we know what will happen next, because we can ask other people who have lived longer than us. But no matter how old we get, we cannot ask anybody what happens after we die. No matter what some fortune-tellers say, we can't talk to dead people. That's why so many people have such different ideas about what happens after we die.

All the major religions teach a very big idea about what happens after we die: Our bodies really die, but something in us keeps on living. Even though all religions do not teach us about God, all religions teach that death is not the end of everything.

The name for the part of us that lives on after death is different for all religions. Jews and Christians call it our *soul*. The ancient Egyptians called the soul *ba*. Hindus call the soul *atman*.

The Zoroastrians call the soul *urvan*. In Islam the soul is called *nafs*, or sometimes *ruh*.

The Arabic word for soul, *ruh*, is the same as the Hebrew word *ruach*, and they both mean "breath" or "spirit." What a great idea, thinking of our souls as like the breath of God in us. When we die, the breath goes out of our body, and so our soul goes out of our body. A soul is the part of us that is good and kind, loving and protecting, curious and caring. And when we are about to do something bad, it's our soul that speaks up and tells us not to do it.

Judaism, Christianity, and Islam teach us that people have souls and animals don't. Hinduism teaches that animals *do* have souls. In fact, Hindus believe that our soul might go into an animal after we die (but only if we are *very* bad and only for a short time). For Jews and Christians and Muslims, this can't happen. They teach that the little piece of God in us, our soul, can't fit into an animal. That does not mean that animals are nothing; it just means that they are not as special as people.

Hindus teach that every living thing has a soul that came from some other living thing. They think that everything has a soul that gets used again and again at the moment when the living thing the soul is in dies. This idea has a big name, *reincarnation*, but what that big word means is just this: Our souls get used again in some other living thing after we die.

Hindus believe that where our used souls get put back depends on how good or bad we were in our last life. If we are real good, our soul could come back as a president or a rock star or a dog in a big house where they cook it hamburgers for dinner. If we are bad we come back as a bug or a gangster. They call this way of being recycled in a better or worse way, depending on how good or bad you are, *karma*. This is why all Buddhists and most Hindus are vegetarians. When you teach that souls get

used again in any animal, it is just not safe to eat anything that might once have taken you to a baseball game. Reincarnation is fun to think about, because you can kick back and imagine what sort of lives you might have lived before the life you are living now.

Judaism, Christianity, and Islam teach that our souls keep living after our bodies die. And where do they live? You guessed it! They live in heaven or hell. Heaven and hell mean pretty much the same thing for Jews, Christians, and Muslims. Heaven is the place where the souls of good people go after the body they were living in dies, and hell is the place where the souls of bad people go.

People wonder a lot what heaven and hell look like, and people wonder even more about how you know if you are good enough for heaven or bad enough for hell. These are big questions, but they can't be answered for sure until after we die and look around, and when that happens there are no telephones to call home and tell folks the news. Even so, all the religions that believe in heaven and hell have mostly the same ideas about what they look like and who gets in.

Hell

What Christians call *hell* (in English) Jews call *gehinnom* (in Hebrew) and Muslims call *jahannam* (in Arabic). Sometimes Muslims call hell "the Fire," which is *al-nar* in Arabic. Fire and hell seem to go together for many people, and there are many teachings that hell is hot. But whatever the temperature of hell, one thing is sure: Hell is no place for good folks.

One of the big questions about hell is whether your soul can get out of hell once it goes in. The answer of most of the religions that believe in hell is: If you get into hell, you are not getting out! You are not passing Go, and you definitely are not collecting $200.

But don't worry. Even though nobody ever gets out of hell, not that many people get in either. The teaching of most all the religions is that hell is a place where only the very worst of the worst people go. Hitler is probably in hell. So what happens to the souls of most of the rest of us? We may be bad, but we are not *that* bad. Some Christians believe that for the in-between people, like most of us, there is a place between heaven and hell that is waiting for our souls. Christians call it *purgatory*. Hindus call this in-between place *narakas*. It is the place where we get punished for the bad things we did, and then, when the punishment is over, we go to heaven with the people who never did much of anything wrong.

For Jews, *gehinnom* is not really hell. It is more like purgatory. Jews don't teach that hell is a place of suffering and fire forever. Jews believe that when you die, your soul goes to a kind of courtroom and there is a trial where God is the judge. God decides what should happen to you. If you were good enough, you go to heaven. If you were really bad, you get iced. Your soul is either wiped out right away or it's held until the Messiah comes, and then you get wiped out. Either way, you're toast. For Jews it's either heaven, which is great, or hell, which is nothing at all, forever.

Heaven

What Christians call *heaven*, Hindus call *svarga*, and Jews call *ha-olam habah*, "the world to come," or sometimes *ha'atid lavo*, "the future to come," or sometimes *gan eden*, "the Garden of Eden."

Jews and Muslims also call heaven *paradise*, which is an English word that comes from a Greek word that comes from a Hebrew word that means the Garden of Eden.

Thinking about heaven as being like the Garden of Eden is neat. It would be kind of like a Disneyland for souls. It would probably be warm and sunny in the daytime, and even though it would be dark at night and full of neat animals, it would not be spooky, and the animals would not want to eat you, and the bugs would not want to fly into your ear or bite you behind your knee. Heaven would probably be a place of peace where you never have to lock your door and you never run out of milk. In heaven, you probably get rid of zits by eating chocolate! *Heaven is just the best!*

There are many beautiful teachings about heaven in the holy books. Lions lying down with lambs, everybody happy and doing the things God gave us the gifts to do. It's a place where we meet again the souls of all the people we loved in this lifetime who died before us. A place where lonely people find friends, a place where hungry people find food, a place where sick people will be well again. The main thing about heaven that comes through in many of the teaching of the religions is that heaven is a place where God is real close all the time!

Ask yourself this question: "Would I do the right thing if there was no heaven and no hell?" If your answer is that you would do every bad thing you could if there was no heaven or hell, then maybe you should think a little more about why you do what you do.

It's okay to want to get to heaven to be near God and to be near everybody you loved when they were alive. Going to heaven is going to be great! Thinking about it will keep you happy when you are sad. It will take away your worries about what happened to the people you loved who died. Heaven really is the teaching of hope. Heaven is knowing that everything will be all right somehow, someday.

If you would like an idea of heaven and hell that is not spooky, try this old story.

Once upon a time a student asked a wise teacher, "What is the difference between heaven and hell?"

The wise teacher answered by saying this: "Hell is a place where all the people are hungry and are sitting around a big table filled with every kind of wonderful food. They can see the food. They can smell the food. They can even reach out and touch the food, but their elbows are locked stiff, so they cannot bring the food to their mouths and eat it. That is hell," said the teacher.

The students said, "Yes, that is hell. And what is heaven like?"

The teacher said, "Oh, heaven. In heaven the people who have lived a good life are hungry, and they are sitting around a big table filled with every kind of wonderful food. They can see the food. They can smell the food. They can even reach out and touch the food, but their elbows are locked stiff, so they cannot bring the food to their mouths and eat it."

The students were confused and asked, "What is the difference between heaven and hell?"

And the teacher answered by saying, "In heaven the people are feeding each other."

CHAPTER 18

What Are Some of the Bad Things in Religions?

Let's face it, nothing is perfect except God, and religion is not God. Religion is just our very best guess about God and about what we think God wants us to do. Religion gets ideas straight from God, and religion also gets ideas from the world. The ideas that religion gets from God are true and perfect and good and right. The problems come from the ideas religions get from the world and put into the religions *as if* God had given them, when really God had nothing to do with the ideas at all. Some of these ideas are *terrible*, and when people hear that religions teach those ideas, they think that the whole religion is terrible.

Now the big question is this: How can we know which ideas come from God and which ideas are just from the world? One way to figure it out is to see how religious people act. If they act in a way that hurts other people or makes them slaves, then we can say those ideas are not from God! But if the religions teach ideas that get people to love each other and make peace and treat everybody with respect, then we can say those ideas are *definitely* from God.

The other important thing to remember about the bad things in religion is that we should not blame a whole religion for what a few bad people in that religion do. Stop and think about this. Sometimes people who say they are a part of a religion do the wrong thing even though the religion teaches them to do the right thing. Is it fair to blame the religion because some of the people in it are jerks? A religion teaches us to do the right thing, just like parents teach us to do the right thing. If we go wrong, it's *our* fault, not theirs. In the same way, just because there are mad scientists and crazy artists does not mean that all of science and art are mad or crazy. Just because there have been people who have, in the name of religion, done bad things—sometimes *very* bad things—does not mean that religions are bad.

But sometimes it's hard to forgive religion for the bad things that people do when the people who do the bad things are big shots in that religion. Take the Crusades. In 1095 Pope Urban the Second said, "God wants us to kill Muslims and Jews who are in our Holy Land." The pope did not understand that that place was holy for Muslims and Jews too. So when the crusaders found Jews, they beat them up, killed some of them, and took their stuff. They also killed a lot of Muslims, who then killed a lot of crusaders.

Even though he was the pope, Urban the Second was a bad guy and a bad Christian. What he did was against the teaching of Jesus and against the teaching of all good Christians. But because he was the boss, the Crusades got started, and lots of people who did nothing wrong got killed. It is things like the Crusades that definitely give religion a bad name. But if you take a look at *all* the popes, and everything they did, there is *much* more good than bad.

What about bad religions? Are there any religions where the people do bad things not because they are making a mistake but because they are doing *exactly* what the religion teaches? Unfortunately the answer is yes, there are bad religions.

Long ago, before the five big religions got started, and even nowadays in faraway places, there were and are bad religions. The way you know they are bad is that they hurt people as a part of the religion. These religions hurt people mostly by killing them to make the gods happy as part of their holy times. There is nothing we can say about this except: Religions that do these bad things as part of the religion are bad religions. We have tried in this book to keep an open mind about what every religion has to teach, but hurting people and killing people in the name of God or religion is *just plain wrong*. The thing to remember is that all the bad religions are small, and most of them are dead and gone. Religions that teach people to hurt each other just can't make it for very long.

There are, however, still some teachings of the big good religions that seem very bad to many people, and we need to talk about some of those teachings too. We do not want you to finish this book and think that just because something is in a religion we are in favor of it. Almost everything in religions is good, but you find some bad teachings here and there. We think that the Hindu caste system is right up there at the top of the list.

The Hindu Caste System

We already explained how Hinduism teaches that people are divided into groups that cannot mix with each other. The caste system started out all right because it was just describing the different jobs people had to do, but then it became bad, because if you were in a low caste there was nothing you could do to get out of it. This was terrible for the people in the low castes—it made them poor, and it made other people look down on them.

Buddha tried to break up the caste system and failed, so he started a new religion where caste did not matter. In modern times, the great Hindu leader Mahatma Gandhi also tried to break up the caste system, and he failed too. Caste is just so deep in the culture of India and Hinduism that it can't be washed out easily. Gandhi was a Hindu who did not believe in caste. We hope someday Hinduism will change and teach that we are all equal and all part of one big happy varna called planet earth.

Religious Fanatics

Nowadays there is a lot of talk about crazy religious people. You've probably heard about Catholics and Protestants killing each other in Northern Ireland, Jews and Muslims killing each other in Israel, Muslims and Orthodox Christians killing each other in Bosnia, Hutus and Tutsis killing each other in Rwanda, and Hindus and Muslims killing each other in India. If you read the papers some days, you might think that lots of religious people own both holy books and guns. These fights give religions a bad name. These fanatics who want to hurt people and who want to bomb places and kill innocent people because of what they think their religion teaches have just plain got their religion wrong!

Cults

Cults are parts of a religion that take away people's brains. Cults try very hard to get people to do exactly what the leaders of the cult tell them to do. Cults make people into robots, into zombies, into blind followers. All the real religions teach people just the opposite. They teach us to think for ourselves and to decide for ourselves to follow the teaching of the religion.

Cults are very dangerous because many of the people in cults don't even know that they've been brainwashed. Most of the time, if someone can be taken away from the cult for a few months and brought back to their parents and friends, that person will snap out of it, and realize that the cult is very dangerous. The person will understand that God wants us to love God without being forced to love God.

Televangelists

If you turn on the TV on Sundays, or most any day now, you can see some guy or gal in a church somewhere praying and singing and leading a nice service. Then all of a sudden they ask you to send in your money. They are asking for money so that they can pay for the television time and so that they can ask you for more money later on. These people are called televangelists. Not all the religious folks on television are televangelists, and not all televangelists are bad. (We are on television sometimes, and we are *great* guys!) Some televangelists are bad because they get a lot of money and don't use the money in the way they say they will. This is just plain stealing, and some televangelists steal money.

Televangelists reach so many millions of people that if even a small part of the millions of viewers send in a few bucks, that can mean millions of dollars coming in. And if nobody keeps an eye on all this money, you can have big problems. When you put money into the collection plate in church or you pay your dues in the synagogue, there are lots of people who watch that money to see that nobody steals it, but when you send money in the mail to some televangelist far away, you have no idea how the money is being used.

Another bad thing about televangelists is that nobody is around to see how the televangelists live. If they take all the money and live like kings and queens in lots of big fancy houses, nobody really knows, because all most people know about tele-vangelists is what they see on TV. If your rabbi or your priest or your minister or your imam suddenly started driving a Ferrari, people in the neighborhood would talk, but people don't see how the televangelists live.

We think that if you have some money to give to a religious place, you should give it to the place down the block. The place down the block is there even after you turn off the television set. When someone you love dies, that minister or priest or rabbi or imam is the one who will bury them and comfort you and pray for you.

Hate

All the real religions in the world teach us to love. They teach us to love God, they teach us to love each other, and they teach us to love the world and all that is in it. But sometimes, religions teach hate. This is one of the worst things in religion.

The teaching of hate takes shape in different ways in the religions that have been poisoned by hate. Some religions teach racism. Racism is hating people because of the color of their skin. Anti-Semitism is hating people because they are Jewish. Some-times there is religious bigotry in which one religion hates an-other religion just because it is different. The important thing is that no religions teach hatred in their holy books. It is sad and true that many religious leaders have taught hatred and say it comes from the holy books, but they are just plain wrong.

In countries like South Africa where racism was a part of the culture, many religious leaders preached every Sunday that God did not want whites and blacks to live together and that God does not think that blacks are as good as whites. In America before the Civil War, many churches taught that God wanted blacks to be slaves. The proof that the Bible does not teach racism is that the slaves would read the story of the Exodus from Egypt and get hope from that Bible story that someday they would be free.

Here is a part of the Quran that shows how Islam teaches that any kind of racism is wrong: "O mankind, behold I have created you that you may come to know each other. Behold the noblest of you in the sight of God is the most righteous." If people would only learn the real teaching of their religion, we would be just fine. The teaching of racism happens in religions, but it is against the true teachings of the religions. And that makes it very bad. Judaism has a teaching that God made only one person (Adam) first because God never wanted people to be able to say in times to come, "My ancestor was better than your ancestor."

CHAPTER 19

What Are Some of the Terrific Things in Religions?

—

Just like we have a list of things we do not like in religion, we also have a list of things we love in religion. This list is *much longer* than the list of things we don't like (we couldn't even fit the whole list into this book). You should think of your own list of things you love about religion. We would like to hear from you so that we can add your list to ours. Here's part of our list of some of the things we think are just terrific in the religions of the world.

Weddings

Weddings are one of the great things of religion. You don't choose to be born, you don't choose when you die, but you *choose* when you want to get married (usually). Choosing to say that you want to spend your life with somebody and trust them and love them just the way God loves and trusts us is great.

At a wedding you get to see two people in love. You see how they look at each other and how they love each other, and you thank God that these two people found each other when there was a big chance that they would miss each other in this world. You get to think about babies and about how they are going to start their own family and about how, God willing, they will be a mom and a dad someday. You get to think about what their kids will look like and what they will be like. You get to hope that when their kids grow up, the man and woman will still love each other the way they did on that day of their wedding. And then you think about how life is only wonderful if it is packed with love, and you thank God for making it all that way.

The Ten Commandments

To be great and long is easy, but to be great and short is nearly impossible. There are many great and long symphonies (Beethoven's 9th is really great and really long), and there are great and long novels. What makes the Ten Commandments so unbelievably great is that they are *really great and really short!*

In case you've forgotten them, here they are (in our translation):

1. THERE IS JUST ONE GOD!
2. DON'T EVEN THINK OF HAVING ANOTHER GOD!
3. NO SWEARING!
4. REST ON THE SABBATH DAY! (THAT'S ONE OUT OF EVERY SEVEN.)
5. DO EXACTLY WHAT YOUR MOM AND DAD TELL YOU TO DO AND DO IT RIGHT

AWAY! (UNLESS WHAT THEY TELL YOU
TO DO IS WRONG.)
6. DON'T MURDER ANYBODY!
7. ONLY MAKE LOVE TO THE PERSON YOU
MARRY!
8. DON'T TAKE STUFF THAT ISN'T YOURS!
9. TELL THE TRUTH!
10. DON'T WANT WHAT OTHER PEOPLE
HAVE JUST BECAUSE THEY HAVE IT!

The 23rd Psalm

Remember how when you fell down and scraped your knee,
your mother kissed it and made it all better? Well, the 23rd
Psalm in the Hebrew Bible is just like a mother's kiss. This
psalm is about death. It does not take away the sadness of death,
just like your mom kissing your knee does not take away the
hurt. It just says, "Don't worry, God is with you all the time, and
God will protect you and love you and care for you. There is no
reason to be afraid."

How do you feel when you hear these words that have made
so many people feel better when they were feeling terrible?

The Lord is my shepherd, I shall not want.
He maketh me to lie down in green pastures:
he leadeth me beside still waters.
He restoreth my soul;
he leadeth me in the paths of righteousness for his name's
sake.
Yea, though I walk through the valley of the shadow of
death,
I will fear no evil:

for thou art with me;
thy rod and thy staff they comfort me.
Thou preparest a table before me in the presence of mine
    enemies:
thou anointest my head with oil: my cup runneth over.
Surely goodness and mercy shall follow me all the days of
    my life:
and I will dwell in the house of the Lord for ever.

The idea that God is our shepherd is a very great idea. God is a very good shepherd, even if we are not very good sheep. Even if we go far away from the place God wants us to be, God is always trying to find us and bring us home to the place of green pastures and still waters. Ahh!

The Torah Scroll

Jews love the Torah. The Torah scroll is dressed in a velvet cover and silver crowns with little bells on them, made to cover the wooden posts that hold the sheepskin scroll. The person who carries the Torah scroll gently lifts it out of the ark and carries it kind of like you carry a baby, walking through the synagogue while people are singing and the silver bells on the Torah are tinkling. As the Torah passes each person, he or she will reach out and touch the Torah and then bring his or her hand back and kiss it where it touched the Torah. That way the Torah is kissing them. The Torah is much more than a scroll. It is the way God has kissed the Jews and the way the Jews have kissed the world.

Meditation

Most of us think that how we breathe and how we think have nothing to do with each other. We know that if we don't breathe at all we can't think at all, but we have lost the truth of how our bodies and our minds work together. Meditation reminds us of that truth. Breathing and sitting, standing up and lying down come naturally to most of us, but Buddhism and Hinduism have really taught us to think about how we breathe and how we sit and stand and lie down. They teach that if we breathe slowly and sit very still, our minds will wash clean, just like dirty dishes in a dishwasher. For thousands of years they have taught us about ways to breathe and sit and stand and lie down that are supposed to make us feel good and clear our minds, and help us understand what really matters. It works. All through the East, people meditate and do slow exercises and breathe in special ways. In China it is called *tai chi.* In India it is called *hatha yoga.* Most of the statues of the Buddha show him sitting in the yoga sitting position called the lotus position. You cross your legs and sit with your back straight and with your fingers touching, and you close your eyes and you breathe slowly.

Meditation is not just a way to help you breathe better, it is a way to help you think better and pray better and live better by breathing better. Breathing right is something very simple and very hard. When you meditate and relax and breathe right and think about what really matters, everything good comes rushing in and everything bad goes rushing out. Try it, you'll like it!

The Amida Buddha

In the year 1253 a huge statue of a Buddha sitting cross-legged in prayer was built in Kamakura, Japan. The Buddha is Amida and is worshiped in Japan and China as the Buddha who has the power to bring people to a place called "the Pure Land," which is paradise. People say a special prayer to the Amida Buddha, *namu amida butsu.* Just saying those words is supposed to help wrap a person in the protection of the Amida Buddha.

What is so great to us about the Amida Buddha is that it is both *so* big and also *so* peaceful. Most things that are that big are kind of scary or make you feel like an ant, but the Amida Buddha is big and makes you feel great. Being there helps you really believe that there is at least as much peace in the world as there is war.

The Cross

The cross is a terrific and very powerful symbol for Christians. Every time a Christian sees the cross, he or she remembers Jesus and believes that Jesus was the Messiah and the son of God who came to earth and died for our sins and rose again and left us all with a teaching of how to love each other the way he loved us.

Our favorite is the plain cross. No plastic or wooden or golden Jesus, just the shape of two lines coming together. One line connects us up and down to God and one line connects us back and forth to each other. The cross we love is a simple wooden cross that reminds us always that we are all connected together in love.

Gothic Cathedrals

In Europe, around the year 1500, builders figured out how to make gothic cathedrals, which are really big churches with lots of space inside. In some of them the ceiling might be over a hundred feet high and the walls might have big stained-glass windows in them.

We hope you will go to one of these great gothic cathedrals on a sunny Sunday morning. Our two favorites are Notre Dame in Paris and Chartres, which is south of Paris. You could go to either one of these cathedrals—or any of the other great ones in France or Germany or England, or even into sort-of-gothic cathedrals like St. John the Divine in New York City or the National Cathedral in Washington, D.C.—on a day with sun flooding in through the big stained-glass windows and washing everything in scarlet and purple and blue and gold. On that kind of golden day watch as the ministers or priests and bishops and maybe even a cardinal walk down the center aisle in their gold or white or red vestments with the choir and the people singing. On such a golden day you will feel the power and the beauty of God and the church and the world and the song and the light, and you will say, "God, I know this all costs a bundle, but it is really beautiful, and I am really happy to know you here."

Muezzins

"Allahu akbar! God is great! I bear witness that there is no god but God. I bear witness that Muhammad is the messenger of God. Come to prayer! Come to contentment! There is no god but God." This is the call to prayer that the Muslim prayer singer, called a muezzin, sings out in Arabic when he goes up into the minaret. It is a great call-to-prayer song, because it reminds Muslims to pray each time the muezzin calls, and that is five times every day. You are in the middle of doing your business and then, all of a sudden, there is a guy singing at and calling to you to remember that God is great. It's good to stop your business and kneel down right where you are and pray to Allah and thank Allah for all your blessings.

Mahatma Gandhi

People hit each other too much. Gandhi taught millions of people that they don't have to hit each other to solve their problems. This is why Gandhi was so terrific. Instead of hitting, he believed in the Hindu teaching of *ahimsa,* which is nonviolence. This is a very hard idea to believe in, but it is also a very beautiful one.

Gandhi's full name was Mohandas Karamchand Gandhi. He was called *Mahatma,* a title used for a person of great wisdom and selflessness. He lived from 1869 to 1948, and he helped more than any other person to make India a free nation. He did it by teaching that hitting was always wrong. Many people have learned nonviolence from Gandhi. His most famous American student was Martin Luther King, Jr.

Rev. Martin Luther King, Jr.

It would have been nice to meet Isaiah. It would have been great to meet Amos or Micah or Jeremiah or Ezekiel. The prophets of the Bible were great men and women who heard God speaking to them and who spoke God's words no matter what happened to them. The words they heard from God told people to "do justice, love mercy, and walk humbly with your God." They said, "Let justice roll down like waters, and righteousness like an ever-flowing stream." These words moved mountains and moved hearts. It would have been nice to hear the prophets, but not very long ago we heard a man who spoke just like them. He spoke with their power and their passion. He spoke with their love, and he spoke with their courage. His name was Martin Luther King, Jr.

Martin Luther King, Jr., helped to change the laws that hurt black people in America and helped America live up to its ideals.

He was a Baptist minister who was the son of a minister. He loved God and he loved people like a minister should, but he also loved justice and freedom the way a prophet should. He reminded us that religion is not just about saying prayers and giving presents. Religion is about fixing the world. Religion is about feeding hungry people and clothing naked people and freeing captive people. Everybody knows that religion should be about these things, but sometimes it takes a man like Martin Luther King, Jr., to really remind us that God wants justice, and after we make justice we can light all the candles we want.

The Dalai Lama

Not being able to live in your homeland is really bad, but not having someone to comfort you while you are in exile is even worse. To the six million Tibetan Buddhists in the world, the Dalai Lama is their hope.

The Dalai Lama is a gentle man with a wonderful sense of humor for a Buddha. Tibetan Buddhists believe that he is the fourteenth reincarnation of the first Dalai Lama, who lived about 600 years ago. He was born Tenzin Gyatso, in 1935, but when he was just five years old, people knew that he was the new Dalai Lama. After the Chinese Communists conquered Tibet in 1950, he stayed there for nine years. Now he lives in India and travels the world giving hope to his people.

This courage and this hope would be enough for us to love this gentle man. What is extra special about him is that he brings hope to nearly everybody he meets. He is so open to the other religions of the world, and he always takes joy in meeting people. From him we have learned that the most important question is *not* "How are we all different?" The most important question is, "How are we all alike?" The only reason why many people in the

West know about Buddhism or care about Buddhism is the Dalai Lama, and the way we see things, that is a very good reason indeed.

Mother Teresa

Every now and then we need to remember what a difference one person can make. This is what Mother Teresa does for us. She is a woman who grew up in Albania and became a nun and decided not to give up on the world. She went to the slums of Calcutta, India, where people have almost nothing. Every day, she washes the sick and feeds the orphan babies, and all the time she is smiling and singing. She is happy because she sees God's face in the face of every person she helps. Some folks who are not used to seeing a living saint say, "She can't be that good; nobody is that good."

But she *is* that good, and Mother Teresa reminds us all that one person can make a big difference in the world.

The Messiah

Fixing the world is real hard work, but if you think you have to do it with no help, then fixing the world is impossible. Messiah is the idea, the teaching, the belief, the *hope* that if we work as hard as we can to fix the world we will have help, God's help. Messiah is hope, hope that everything will get fixed here somehow, someday. In this way the belief in the Messiah is one of the best things in religion.

In another way the belief in the Messiah is one of the worst things in religion. The argument about who is the Messiah has divided religions for thousands of years. This argument about the Messiah is what made Christianity split off from Judaism.

Christians and Jews have been arguing about it ever since. Muslims were also a part of the argument. Muslims too did not believe that Jesus was the Messiah, but Christians and Jews argued the most because they lived close to each other. The weird thing is that this argument has been going on for almost two thousand years. Nobody has won, and nobody has given up.

Heaven

Knowing that death is not the end of us is one of the great things that all the religions help us to know. In fact, knowing that death is not the end of us is one of the *only* things that *all* the religions of the world teach.

You know that after you die there is either something waiting for you or nothing waiting for you. You know that your body goes back to be a part of the earth, and it is your soul that goes to heaven. It is really a good thing that it is just your soul that goes to heaven and not your body, because if your body went there too, heaven would be a really crowded place.

Anyway, heaven is one of the very greatest things about religion because believing that our souls are going to heaven gives us two things that everybody needs to live a good life here on planet earth: Heaven gives us hope that everything will turn out all right, and heaven helps us not to be afraid of death.

Heaven gives us hope that everything will turn out all right because it reminds us that the love that begins in this world will continue into the world to come. Heaven gives us hope that the things we have tried all our life to get done here will get done there—and we don't mean getting your room cleaned up, we mean getting everybody to be nice and getting everybody to help out when they can. Heaven also gives us hope that all the really bad people who spend their lives hurting and killing will be stopped forever, and the people who have spent their lives help-ing others will be helped to do that forever.

The second thing that heaven does is to help us not to be afraid of death. There are two kinds of being afraid of death. The first kind of being afraid is being afraid of our own death. The second kind of being afraid is being afraid that someone we love will die. Of course we all die sometime. It is very sad to think of being taken away from this world, but at least we have another world to go to where there is no death and no pain. And besides, in heaven our souls will be with the souls of all our fam-ily who have died before us. We will never be alone, and we will always be loved.

Heaven is the place where we finally learn how to spell God.